Evaluation Methods in Research

Judith Bennett

LONDON • NEW YORK

MT

Continuum

The Tower Building   80 Maiden Lane
11 York Road   Suite 704
London SE1 7NX   New York, NY 10038

British Library Cataloguing-in-Publication Data
A catalogue record for this book is available from the British Library.

ISBN: 0 8264 6478 5 (paperback)

Typeset by RefineCatch Limited, Bungay, Suffolk
Printed and bound in Great Britain by MPG Books Ltd, Bodmin, Cornwall

6\12\08

Contents

Introduction

I came across the diagram reproduced in Figure 1 many years ago in the in-house magazine produced by the company for which my father worked. For me, the story it tells has many parallels with the process of innovation in education! It also highlights why evaluation – the asking of questions to inform decision-making – has a key role to play in any innovation.

About this book

This book is intended to provide both background on the ideas and theories which underpin educational evaluation, and practical guidance on how to plan and undertake an evaluation. It will also argue the case for evaluation being most effective when a *multi-method approach* is adopted: in other words, an approach that draws on a variety of perspectives on evaluation and also employs a range of research strategies and techniques to gather different forms of data.

The book is divided into six main sections. *Section 1* looks at the various ways in which people have defined and explained evaluation, and explores the links between evaluation and research. *Section 2* considers a variety of models and approaches to evaluation. In *Section 3*, models of change which have emerged from evaluation studies are explored. *Section 4* looks at the research strategies and techniques which are employed in evaluation. *Section 5* considers the practicalities of planning

THE SWING PROJECT ......

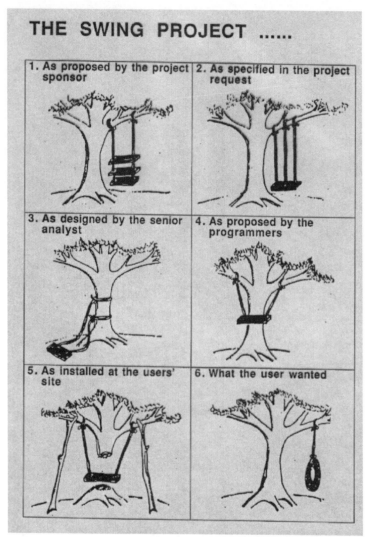

Figure 1 Why evaluation might be important!

an evaluation, focusing on a number of key questions which need to be addressed. Finally, in *Section 6*, three examples of evaluations are presented and discussed, illustrating how principles have been put into practice.

Any book on evaluation needs to address the issue of how far details of general aspects of research methods should be included. In this instance, the decision has been made to include information about key research strategies and techniques, as these are central to the planning and design of an evaluation, but to exclude material on aspects of research methods which are covered in detail in a number of other texts. Thus, matters to do with the detail of designing research instruments (questionnaires, interview schedules, observation schedules) and data analysis are not included in this book. However, the *Appendix* gives details of further reading on research methods, and a *Glossary* has been included for those who may be less familiar with some of the terms used in educational research and evaluation.

If you are reading this book, you are likely to be involved in an educational innovation, and asking one or more of the following questions: *What works? How does it work? How can it be made to work better?* I hope what you read here helps you in your quest to find the answers.

1

What is Educational Evaluation?

This section looks at:

- the terminology associated with educational evaluation;
- ways in which people have defined and explained educational evaluation;
- the reasons why educational evaluation is undertaken;
- the audiences for educational evaluation;
- dimensions of educational evaluation;
- links between evaluation and research.

Introduction: Definitions and terminology

Most people with an interest in education are likely to agree that it is very important to link evaluation to innovation in education. So what is evaluation all about? Box 1.1 illustrates some of the ways in which evaluation has been defined or explained in the context of education.

The statements in Box 1.1 suggest several things about evaluation:

- People use different terminology when they are talking about evaluation.
- People have different perspectives on the nature and purpose of evaluation.
- There has been ongoing debate for several decades over the nature and purpose of evaluation.

Box 1.1 What is evaluation?

- The process of determining to what extent educational objectives are being realized by the programme of curriculum and instruction (Tyler, 1949, 105–6).
- The collection and use of information to make decisions about an educational programme (Cronbach, 1963, 672).
- Its purpose is to see whether curriculum objectives are being, or have been, achieved (Kerr, 1968, 21).
- Evaluation is concerned with securing evidence on the attainment of specific objectives of instruction (Bloom, 1970, 28).
- Curriculum evaluation refers to the process or processes used to weigh the relative merits of those educational alternatives which, at any given time, are deemed to fall within the domain of curriculum practice (Hamilton, 1976, 4).
- Educational evaluation is the process of delineating, obtaining and providing useful information for judging decision alternatives (Jenkins, 1976, 6).
- Evaluation as illumination (Parlett and Hamilton, 1976, 84).
- [Evaluation is] systematic examination of events occurring in and consequent on a contemporary programme – an examination conducted to assist in improving this programme and other programmes having the same general purpose (Cronbach *et al.*, 1980, 14).
- Evaluation [is] the assessment of merit or worth (Nevo, 1986, 16).
- Evaluation can provide a means for translating an educational idea into practice as well as monitoring and enhancing curriculum development (Hopkins, 1989, 3).
- Educational evaluation is about social planning and control (Norris, 1990, 16).
- Evaluators are interested in discerning the effects of interventions over-and-above what could have been expected if the intervention had not been applied (Davies *et al.*, 2000, 253).

Before considering in more detail what evaluation involves, it is useful to look briefly at the sort of terminology people use when talking about it.

Evaluation terminology

There is considerable variety in the terms people use when talking about aspects of evaluation. Evaluation itself may variously and interchangeably be described as educational evaluation, curriculum evaluation, or program(me) evaluation, with the last term being more common in the USA.

Several terms may also be used to describe the change in provision which is being evaluated. These include curriculum development, program(me) development, program(me) implementation, curriculum innovation, innovation, curriculum intervention, intervention or intervention strategies. Again, these terms are interchangeable. The policy normally followed in this book is to use the terms 'evaluation' or 'educational evaluation', and to refer to changes in provision as 'innovations' or 'new programmes'. However, where the work of particular authors is described, the terms used in their original works have been retained.

What is evaluation?

Almost all the statements in Box 1.1 have in common the notions that evaluation involves learning about a new programme through gathering information, and that this information should be linked to decision-making. The information gathered might include the scores students achieve on tests, other measures of cognitive abilities, measures of attitudes, data from observations, and questionnaire and interview data from students, teachers and others associated with the programme. The statements tend to differ in their view of which aspects of such data should be emphasized, and the purposes to which it should be put. The earlier statements, such as those of Tyler (1949) and Kerr (1968), talk in terms of *making judgements* about the extent to which the objectives of a new programme have been achieved, whilst later ones, such as those of Jenkins (1976) and Parlett and Hamilton (1976), see *learning from the process of introducing a new programme* as an important element of evaluation. The most recent (Davies *et al.*, 2000) hints at a return to the ideas underpinning the views expressed in the earlier statements, and indicates that there is ongoing debate over where the balance lies between the learning and judging dimensions of evaluation.

For the purposes of this book, evaluation has been taken to involve the following:

- a focus on the introduction of a new programme;
- collecting and analysing empirical data;
- reaching some form of conclusions or judgements about the data;
- communicating these findings to an audience;
- using the findings to inform decision-making.

Why undertake evaluation?

As the statements in Box 1.1 indicate, evaluation may be undertaken for a variety of purposes. The two main reasons are to determine the effectiveness of a new programme once it has been implemented, and to gather information for improving the programme as it is being developed. However, the information gathered through an evaluation can be used in a number of ways. Cronbach (1963) has suggested it serves three important purposes by informing course improvement, decisions about individuals, and administrative regulation. He explains these as follows:

Course improvement: deciding what instructional materials and methods are satisfactory and where change is needed.

7

Decisions about individuals: identifying the needs of the pupil for the sake of planning his instruction, judging pupil merit for purposes of selection and grouping, acquainting the pupil with his own progress and deficiencies

Administrative regulation: judging how good the school system is, how good individual teachers are, etc.

(1963, 232)

This book is primarily concerned with the first of these purposes – looking at the ways in which the techniques of evaluation can be used to assess the effects of changes in the curriculum and thus to make decisions about how classroom practice might be improved.

Who is evaluation for?

Ultimately, it could be argued, evaluation is for the students in the classrooms, in order to provide them with the best possible educational experiences. However, the audiences for evaluation reports are normally one or more groups of decision-makers who can influence what happens in class-rooms. These groups include the people who have developed a new programme, the people using the programme, and external agencies and other interested parties such as the people who have sponsored the programme, educational researchers and those responsible for curriculum policy or developing new programmes.

Each of the groups interested in an evaluation is likely to have different, although overlapping, priorities and purposes for its outcomes. Those developing the programme will want to know how it is working and what factors appear to help it to work in as many locations as possible. They are also likely to want or need to gather information for the project sponsors, to help persuade other potential users to adopt the programme and to share what they have learned with others involved in developing new programmes. Users will want to know how the programme is working in their particular location, and how this compares with other approaches they may have used, and how their experience compares with that in other locations. They will also want to let the developers know their views on the programme, and share their experiences with other users. Those sponsoring the programme will be concerned with its effects and also that they are getting 'value for money'. Other people involved in developing new programmes will be interested in what they can learn which might be of use in their own work. Policy-makers will want to know what messages emerge from the evaluation which can usefully inform curriculum planning and legislation.

Dimensions of evaluation

Attempts to define evaluation point to a number of different dimensions by which it can characterized. A useful description of these has been developed by Stake (1986), who identified eight different possible dimensions to evaluation studies. These are:

formative-summative
formal-informal
case particular-generalization
product-process
descriptive-judgemental
preordinate-responsive
holistic-analytic
internal-external

(1986, 245-8)

Formative-summative

These two terms are frequently applied to evaluation. A study which is primarily seeking to gather information on the effectiveness of a programme after it has been implemented

9

is termed a summative evaluation (sometimes also called an *outcome* or *impact evaluation*). A summative evaluation seeks answers to questions about what relationships exist between the goals of the programme and its outcomes. A study which is primarily seeking to gather information during the process of implementation, with a view to informing the development of the programme, is called a formative evaluation (sometimes also called a *process* or *progress evaluation*). A formative evaluation seeks answers to questions about the process of implementation and how this relates to the achieved curriculum.

Formal-informal

Stake suggests that informal evaluation is 'a universal and abiding human act, scarcely separable from thinking and feeling' – in other words, people are doing it all the time. Formal evaluation of a programme, however, needs to be systematic, because its findings will be scrutinized and therefore need to be accurate, reliable, credible and of use to those involved.

Case particular-generalization

The findings of an evaluation of a particular programme may only apply to that programme specifically, or they may apply to other programmes which share similar approaches and features. If the aim of an evaluation is to permit generalizations to be made, then there is a much greater need for careful controls and description to provide a secure basis for these generalizations.

Product-process

Some evaluations focus primarily on the outcomes of a programme, whilst others focus on the processes which gave rise to these outcomes. Product-oriented evaluation tends to provide information about *what* effects are associated with a particular programme, and process-oriented evaluation yields information about *why* those effects occurred.

Descriptive-judgemental

The judgemental dimension of evaluation is evident in many of the statements in Box 1.1. Most evaluation studies aim to provide a balance between description and judgement.

Preordinate-responsive

This dimension concerns the extent to which the evaluation agenda takes account of the concerns of those involved in the programme. A preordinate study will focus on the objectives of the programme and the evaluation will be designed to assess the extent to which these objectives have been realized. A responsive study permits some of the agenda to be set by those involved in the programme, and allows for issues to be explored as they emerge during the evaluation. It also permits unanticipated outcomes to be identified.

Holistic-analytic

Some evaluations consider the programme as a whole, often using case studies to document and explore complex inter-actions. Others focus on particular key aspects of a programme and examine the links between particular variables.

Internal-external

Some evaluations are undertaken by people involved in the development of a new programme, whilst others appoint external evaluators. External evaluations tend to be seen as more 'objective', although internal evaluations have the advantage of allowing the developers to focus on what they see as the key features of the programme which need to be explored.

These eight dimensions point to the diversity which can exist in evaluation. Key questions likely to influence the nature of an evaluation concern who the evaluation is for and what purposes it is to serve. It is also the case that decisions made about positions on one particular dimension are likely to determine positions on other dimensions. For example, a summative evaluation is likely to be preordinate in nature, to focus on the products and to be undertaken by an external evaluator. In contrast, an internal evaluation is likely to be formative and look at processes.

What is the relationship between evaluation and research?

It is clear from the discussion so far that evaluation has links with educational research. A number of authors have explored the relationship between the two, with a variety of views being expressed about areas of overlap and difference. Norris (1990) suggests:

> It is generally assumed that evaluation is the application of research methods to elucidate a problem of action. Looked at in this way, evaluation is not strikingly different from research ... Evaluation is an extension of research, sharing its methods and methodology and demanding similar skills and qualities from its practitioners.
>
> (1990, 97)

This view contrasts with that of MacDonald (1976), who sees

> ... research as a branch of evaluation – a branch whose task it is to solve the technological problems encountered by the evaluator.
>
> (1976, 132)

Whilst both Norris and MacDonald appear to see research and evaluation as closely linked, others have suggested they are more clearly distinct. For example, Smith and Glass (1987) identify eight characteristics which they see as distinguishing research from evaluation. These are summarized in Table 1.1.

An important point to make about the distinctions between research and evaluation summarized in Table 1.1 is that they represent an *ideal*, and what happens in practice may be rather different. As Smith and Glass point out, the distinctions between research and evaluation may become blurred. Two ways in which they suggest this might happen concern the 'value-free' nature of research, and the findings of evaluation studies. Research is rarely as value-free as it might aspire to be, as researchers inevitably bring their own interests, motivations and agenda to research studies. It is also the case that an evaluation study, although focusing on one particular programme, may generate findings that are of much wider interest and applicability, thus contributing to knowledge more generally.

Another view on the relationship between research and evaluation is given by Laurence Stenhouse in his influential book, *An Introduction to Curriculum Research and Development*:

> Evaluation should, as it were, lead development and be integrated with it. Then the conceptual distinction between development and evaluation is destroyed and the two merge as research.
>
> (1975, 122)

From the variety of views that has been expressed, it is clear that there is considerable overlap between research and evaluation, although people may have different opinions on the degree of overlaps. In part, these views arise from different interpretations of the word 'research'. It is normally described in terms which suggest that its aim is the pursuit of new knowledge and, as such, it can take a number of different forms. One type of research – often called *pure* or, more colloquially, 'blue skies' research – is open-ended and exploratory, seeking new patterns, explanations and theories. This type of research is clearly distinct from evaluation, and is generally more closely associated with the natural sciences than with educational research.

Norris (1990) suggests that one of the problems with attempts to delineate differences between research and evaluation arises from a narrow view of research which

Table 1.1 Ways in which research and evaluation may differ

Characteristic	Research	Evaluation
1 The intent and purpose of the study	To 'advance the frontiers of knowledge, to gain general understanding about the phenomena being studied'	To gather information to judge the value and merit of a specific innovation (or 'parochial', in the words of Smith and Glass), and to inform decisions
2 The scope of the study	May have a narrow focus	More comprehensive
3 The agenda of the study	Set by the researcher	Set by the client commissioning the evaluation
4 The origins of the study	Arises from 'curiosity and the researcher's need to know'	Arises from a client commissioning the evaluation
5 Accountability	To the research community	To the client who commissioned the evaluation
6 Timeliness	Can take place at any time	Takes place when a problem arises or a decision needs to be reached.
7 Values	Aspires to neutrality in values	Must represent the multiple values of the various interested groups
8 Criteria for judging study	Internal and external validity	Utility and credibility

Adapted from Smith and Glass, 1987, 33–8.

> . . . ignores the social context of educational enquiry, the hierarchic nature of research communities, the reward structure of universities, the role of central governments in supporting certain projects and not others, and the long established relationship between social research and reform.
>
> (1990, 99)

Pure research is often distinguished from a second type, called *applied* research, which involves the testing of theories and hypotheses. Here, the distinction between research and evaluation is less clear-cut, as it could be argued that any new programme aimed at improving practice is a hypothesis about teaching, and evaluation involves testing that hypothesis.

Whatever conclusions people reach about the relationship between evaluation and research, those undertaking evaluation will inevitably need to draw on the strategies and techniques of research if they want to gather systematic evidence to help answer many of the questions they will be asking.

Summary

This section has provided some of the background to evaluation, and pointed to issues and areas of debate. These are explored in more detail in the following sections. In particular, it has shown that:

- there are various views on the nature and purpose of evaluation;
- there are several different potential audiences for evaluation, each with their own priorities;
- evaluation may be characterized in a number of different ways;
- the distinction between evaluation and research is not clear-cut, but evaluation forms an important area of research in education.

2

Models and Approaches in Educational Evaluation

This section looks at:

- general ideas about the approaches and models used in educational evaluation;
- key features of particular evaluation approaches and models, including the classical approach as exemplified by Ralph Tyler's 'objectives model' and the 'illuminative evaluation' approach of David Parlett and Malcolm Hamilton;
- ways of characterizing research and evaluation questions;
- the politics of educational evaluation;
- recent trends and developments in educational evaluation, including randomized controlled trials (RCTs) and design experiments.

Approaches and models in educational evaluation

Two general points are worth making before looking in more detail at ways of approaching evaluation. First, many attempts have been made to summarize and describe approaches and models in educational evaluation. Whilst there are significant differences between some of the approaches and models, others overlap to a greater or lesser extent. Thus, these summaries and overviews tend to cover much the same ground in slightly different ways. Second, summaries of approaches and models often present ideal cases or oversimplifications of what actually happens. In practice, evaluators generally recognize the strengths and limitations of individual approaches and the majority of evaluation studies therefore draw on more than one approach or model. Nonetheless, these summaries are useful in providing an overview of the terminology, key features and issues which need to be considered when planning an evaluation study.

Approaches or models?

The literature tends to use these terms interchangeably. The term 'model' is often used to describe an approach which has been developed by a particular person. Thus, for example, reference is made to 'the Tyler objectives model' or 'Stake's countenance model'. (These, together with other models, are described in more detail later in this section.) These models of educational evaluation are characterized by a specific approach to evaluation design or to a particular set of circumstances to be evaluated.

Two overviews

Lawton (1980, 1983) in the UK and Stake (1986) in the USA have both attempted to pull together the diversity of approaches used in educational evaluation studies. The structure, emphasis and terminology of the overviews reflect the different traditions and ways in which educational evaluation has developed in each of these countries. (More detail about the development of educational evaluation in the USA and the UK may be found in Norris, 1990.)

Lawton (1980, 1983) developed a taxonomy of six models of educational evaluation:

1 The classical (or 'agricultural botany') research model
2 The research and development (R and D) (or industrial factory) model
3 The illuminative (or anthropological) model
4 The briefing decision-makers (or political) model

17

5 The teacher-as-researcher (or professional) model
6 The case study (or portrayal) model

Lawton indicates that the order in which these models are listed roughly follows the order in which they were developed, although he acknowledges there are areas of overlap. Some of these models are associated with particular approaches. For example, the classical and research and development models are likely to adopt an experimental approach to evaluation such as is associated with the work of Tyler (1949), involving control groups and pre- and post-testing, whereas the illuminative model uses the more descriptive approaches originally developed by Parlett and Hamilton (1972, 1976) and often takes the form of a case study.

Stake (1986) identified nine approaches to evaluation. These are:

1 Student gain by testing – to measure student performance and progress
2 Institutional self-study by staff – to review and increase staff effectiveness
3 Blue-ribbon panel – to resolve crises and preserve the institution
4 Transaction–observation – to provide understanding of activities
5 Management analysis – to increase rationality in day-to-day decisions
6 Instructional research – to generate explanations and tactics of instruction
7 Social policy analysis – to aid development of institutional policies
8 Goal-free evaluation – to assess the effects of a programme
9 Adversary evaluation – to resolve a two-option choice

Table 2.1 summarizes the key features of these approaches, as outlined by Stake (1986, where fuller description and elaboration may be found). Stake also notes that the descriptions are over-simplifications and that there is overlap. The table is detailed (and it is not necessary to absorb all the detail), but helpful in gaining a feel for some of the key ideas and terminology associated with educational evaluation.

Although the summaries of Lawton and Stake have different structure and terminology, both, it could be argued, have just two principal models (or paradigms) which could be described as distinctly different: the classical research model and illuminative evaluation. Oakley (2000), in discussing what she terms the 'paradigm wars' in educational research and evaluation, has produced a useful summary of the chief characteristics of the two prevailing methodological paradigms which may be found in Table 2.2. As with Stake's overview, absorbing the detail of this table is less necessary than getting a feel for the key ideas and terminology. As the next section will demonstrate, the classical research model of evaluation reflects many of the characteristics Oakley has associated with what she terms the 'logical positivist/scientific' paradigm, whilst the characteristics of the 'naturalist/interpretivist' paradigm are much closer to those of illuminative evaluation. The next section considers these two main models in more detail, together with briefer descriptions of other approaches to evaluation.

The classical research model

The classical research model sees the evaluation of a programme as being similar to that of a standard scientific experiment involving the testing of a hypothesis. In its simplest form, an experiment involves testing a hypothesis by making a change in the value of one variable (called the independent variable) and observing the effect of that change on another variable (the dependent variable). In educational contexts, the hypothesis being tested is that a particular intervention, in the form of a new programme, will result in a particular outcome. The model involves four main steps:

1 two groups of students, one a control group and one an experimental group, are tested on a particular part of their programme;

19

Table 2.1 Stake's nine approaches to educational evaluation

Approach	Purpose	Key elements	Some key protagonists	Risks	Payoffs
Student gain by testing	To measure student performance and progress	Goal statements; test score analysis; discrepancy between goal and actuality	Ralph Tyler	Over-simplify educational aims; ignore processes	Emphasize, ascertain student progress
Institutional self-study by staff	To review and increase staff effectiveness	Committee work; standards set by staff; discussion; professionalism		Alienate some staff; ignore values of outsiders	Increase staff awareness, sense of responsibility
Blue-ribbon panel	To resolve crises and preserve the institution	Prestigious panel; the visit; review of existing data and documents		Postpone action; over-rely on intuition	Gather best insights, judgement
Transaction observation	To provide understanding of activities and values	Educational issues; classroom observation; case studies; pluralism	Malcolm Parlett and David Hamilton; Robert Stake	Over-rely on subjective perceptions; ignore causes	Produce broad picture of programme; see conflict in values

	To increase rationality in day-to-day decisions	Lists of options; estimates; feedback loops; costs; efficiency		Over-value efficiency; undervalue implicits	Feedback for decision making
Management analysis					
Instructional research	To generate explanations and tactics of instruction	Controlled conditions, multivariate analysis; bases for generalization		Artificial conditions; ignore the humanistic	New principles of teaching and materials development
Social policy analysis	To aid development of institutional policies	Measures of social conditions and administrative implementation		Neglect of educational issues, details	Social choices, constraints clarified
Goal-free evaluation	To assess effects of programme	Ignore proponent claims, follow checklist	Michael Scriven	Over-value documents and record keeping	Data on effect with little cooption
Adversary evaluation	To resolve a two-option choice	Opposing advocates, cross-examination, the jury		Personalistic, superficial, time-bound	Information on impact is good; claims put to test

Adapted from Stake, 1986, 252–3.

Table 2.2 Oakley's summary of the two main paradigms of educational research and evaluation

	'(logical) positivist'/'scientific'/'quantitative'/'positivism'	'naturalist'/'interpretivist'/'qualitative'
Aims	Testing hypotheses/generalizing	Generating hypotheses/describing
Purpose	Verification	Discovery
Approach	Top-down	Bottom-up
Preferred technique	Quantitative	Qualitative
Research strategy	Structured	Unstructured
Stance	Reductionist/inferential/hypothetico-deductive/outcome-oriented/exclusively rational/oriented to prediction and control	Expansionist/exploratory/inductive/process-oriented/rational and intuitive/oriented to understanding
Method	Counting/obtrusive and controlled measurement (surveys, experiments, case control studies, statistical records, structured observations, content analysis)	Observing (participant observation, in-depth interviewing, action research, case studies, life history methods, focus groups)
Implementation of method	Decided *a priori*	Decided in field setting
Values	Value-free	Value-bound
Instrument	Physical device/pencil and paper	The researcher
Researcher's stance	Outsider	Insider
Relationship of researcher and subject	Distant/independent	Close/interactive and inseparable

	'Laboratory'	'Nature'
Setting		
Data	Hard, reliable, replicable	Rich, deep, valid
Data type	Report of attitudes and actions	Feeling, behaviour, thoughts, actions as experienced or witnessed
Data analysis	Specified in advance	Worked out during the study
Analytic units	Predefined variables	Patterns and natural events
Quality criterion	Rigour/proof/evidence/statistical significance	Relevance/plausibility/illustrativeness/responsiveness to subjects' experiences
Source of theory	*A priori*	Grounded
Relationship between theory and research	Confirmation	Emergent
Causal links	Real causes exist	Causes and effects cannot be distinguished
Nature of truth statements	Time- and context-free generalizations are possible	Only time- and context-bound working hypotheses are possible
Image of reality	Singular/tangible/fragmentable/static/external	Multiple/holistic/dynamic/socially-constructed
Research product	Stresses validity of research findings for scholarly community	Stresses meaningfulness of research findings to scholarly and user communities

Taken from Oakley, 2000, 26–7.

2 some form of educational 'treatment', such as a new teaching technique, is applied to the experimental group;
3 both groups are retested;
4 the performance of the groups is compared to assess the effects of the treatment.

Central to the classical research model is the notion that the aims of the programme can be translated into specific objectives, or intended learning outcomes, which can be measured. The model also places a premium on the reliability and validity of data collected.

What Lawton calls the research and development (R & D) model is a variant of the classical model and parallels evaluation with the industrial process of improving a product through testing. As in the classical model, specific, measurable objectives are developed from the aims and tests devised to assess these. The tests are administered before and after the new programme is used in order to assess its effects. The R & D model does not always use control groups.

Ralph Tyler: the 'objectives' model of evaluation

The classical research model is closely associated with the work of Ralph Tyler in the USA, and most accounts of the development of educational evaluation begin with his highly influential work. Tyler was critical of what he saw as the very unsystematic approach adopted in curriculum development in the USA in the 1940s. In 1949, he published his book *The Basic Principles of Curriculum and Instruction* (Tyler, 1949), in which he proposed four basic questions which, he argued, were central to curriculum planning and evaluation.

1 What educational purposes should the school seek to attain?
2 What educational experiences can be provided that are likely to attain these purposes?
3 How can these educational experiences be effectively organized?
4 How can we determine whether these purposes are being attained? (1949, 1)

These questions can be summarized as a four-step sequence

objectives → content → organization → evaluation

with, as the first quotation in Box 1.1 says, educational evaluation then being

> ... the process of determining to what extent the educational objectives are realized by the program of curriculum and instruction.
>
> (1949, 105–6)

This model is often referred to as the 'objectives model' of evaluation, and it has had a significant impact on educational evaluation. Certainly, the apparent simplicity of a model which seeks to compare actual effects with declared goals has its attractions. It also seems reasonable to suggest, as Tyler does, that any new educational programme should have clearly stated objectives, and there should be general agreement over how these can be recognized and measured for the purposes of evaluation. The objectives model underpinned the evaluation of much curriculum development in the USA in the 1960s and 1970s, when its influence was also felt in the UK and elsewhere. From the policy-makers' perspective, the classical model of evaluation appears to provide an answer to the question, 'what works?'

The classical model has been criticized for a number of reasons. First, it does not take account of the complexity of people's behaviour and the dynamics in teaching and learning situations. The critical label of 'agricultural–botany approach' was applied to the classical model by Parlett and Hamilton (1972, 1976) because of its failure to address differences between the behaviour of humans and plants. As Lawton (1980) put it: 'human beings perform differently when under observation, cabbages do not' (112). Second, educational settings involve a number of variables, not all of which can be easily controlled. Third, the model tends to focus on what can be measured and easily quantified, and an evaluation which focuses solely on these aspects runs the risk of missing other unplanned outcomes which may be of importance. A final criticism is that the objectives model focuses on inputs and outputs, and treats the classroom as a 'black box'. This means that the findings are of limited use because they only demonstrate *what* has happened, and do not explain *why* it happened.

One outcome of these criticisms has been an exploration of variations on the experimental design which may be more appropriate to educational settings (see, for example, Fitz-Gibbon and Morris, 1987). A second, more radical, outcome has been the rejection of experimental approaches and the proposal of alternative ways of undertaking evaluation.

The illuminative evaluation model

Malcolm Parlett and David Hamilton: illuminative evaluation

The early 1970s saw the emergence of a new style of educational evaluation, whose proponents were highly critical of the classical model of evaluation. In the UK, in their very influential paper '*Evaluation as illumination: A new approach to the study of innovative programmes*', Malcolm Parlett and David Hamilton (Parlett and Hamilton, 1972, 1976) argued strongly against classical approaches to evaluation, saying that the notion of matching groups for experimental purposes is impossible in educational settings, first, because there are so many potentially important variables that would need to be controlled, and second, because it is impossible to determine in advance what all the relevant variables might be in any particular situation. Parlett and Hamilton proposed an alternative approach which they termed 'illuminative evaluation', drawing on the methods of social anthropology to study innovations in context and without the need for parallel control groups. Such an approach, they contend

> . . . takes account of the wider contexts in which educational innovations function . . . its primary concern is

with description and interpretation rather than measurement and prediction.

(1976, 88)

Thus, in contrast to the classical research model, which sets out to gather data to enable an hypothesis to be tested, illuminative evaluation seeks to generate hypotheses and theories from within the data which have been gathered.

Parlett and Hamilton identify two key concepts in illuminative evaluation, the instructional system and the learning milieu. The *instructional system* is what they call a 'catalogue description' or an idealized specification of a programme which includes a set of pedagogic assumptions (assumptions about teaching and learning) and details of techniques and equipment. In classical evaluation, the objectives are extracted from this catalogue, and instruments devised to assess the extent to which they have been realized. Parlett and Hamilton are critical of this approach:

> This technological approach fails to recognize the catalogue description for what it is. It ignores the fact that an instructional system, when adopted, undergoes modifications that are rarely trivial. The instructional system ... assumes a different form in every situation ... as teachers, administrators, technicians and students interpret and reinterpret the instructional system for their particular setting.
>
> (1976, 89–90)

The *learning milieu* is the network of cultural, social, institutional and psychological factors which affect the environment in which students and teachers work together. Parlett and Hamilton argue that that the concept of the learning milieu is central to evaluation as it is necessary for analyzing the interdependence of learning and teaching, and for relating the organization and practices of instruction to the immediate and long-term responses of students.

Parlett and Hamilton go on to propose a three-phase model

of educational evaluation which involves progressive focusing through observation, further inquiry, and seeking explanations. The first phase involves relatively open-ended data collection in order to identify issues, the second is a more focused phase in which these issues are explored in more detail, and the last phase involves looking for patterns and explanations in the data. They recommend drawing on four sources of evidence: observation of events to identify common incidents, recurring trends and issues; interviews with participants to probe their views; questionnaire and test data where appropriate, and documentary and other background information to set the innovation in context. Whilst they do not reject quantitative data completely, they see it as less important and informative than qualitative data. The outcome of the evaluation is a detailed case study of the programme in use.

Although illuminative evaluation has strong appeal, there are several potential drawbacks to the approach. It raises a number of methodological issues, particularly in relation to its use of case studies. A key issue concerns the influence that those conducting an evaluation have over the nature of the data collected, and questions the reliability and validity of the data and the extent to which both the data and the interpretation are 'objective' rather than reflecting the views of the evaluators. In order to minimize these concerns, case studies make use of triangulation (i.e. drawing on multiple data sources) in data collection and the stages in analysis are made transparent through the use of data audit trails (i.e. summaries of all the steps taken in collecting and analysing data). A second issue concerns the extent to which the findings of a case study can be generalized. Those who make use of case studies also see other aspects such as 'trustworthiness' (Lincoln and Guba, 1985) and 'relatability' (Bassey, 1981) as of more central importance than reliability, validity and generalizability. In other words, a good case study will be reported in such a way that the members of a similar group will find it credible, be able to identify with the problems and issues being reported, and draw on these to see ways of solving similar problems in their own situation.

Illuminative evaluation has also been subjected to strong criticism. For example, Delamont (1978) and Atkinson and Delamont (1993) suggest that illuminative evaluation is as limited as classical evaluation in that

> Without an adequately formulated body of theory or methods, the illuminators have been, and will be, unable to progress and generate a coherent, cumulative research tradition. They cannot transcend the short-term practicalities of any given programme of curriculum innovation. They merely substitute one variety of atheoretical 'findings' – based mainly on observation and interview – for another – based mainly on test scores.
>
> (1993, 218)

Despite the potential drawbacks and criticism, many have seen the flexibility of the illuminative evaluation approach as being particularly relevant to educational contexts and, as such, it became increasingly popular in the 1970s and 1980s.

Other models of evaluation

The classical research model and illuminative evaluation illustrate two very contrasting approaches to evaluation. However, other approaches have also been advocated, a number of which combine aspects of both approaches.

Robert Stake: the countenance model

Robert Stake's model of evaluation (Stake, 1967) emerged from a concern over the narrowness and limitations of the classical method, particularly as it was being used in the USA. Though not as critical of the classical approach as Parlett and Hamilton, Stake felt that the classical method moved too quickly to detailed measurements at the expense of taking in the broader context of the situation being evaluated. He therefore argued for a model of evaluation which broadened the field of data which was eligible (or, to use his term, could be *countenanced*) for collection during an evaluation. Such data should include descriptive aspects which he termed *antecedent, transaction* and *outcome* data. Antecedents are conditions which exist prior to the introduction of a programme and may affect its outcomes, transactions are what actually takes place in the teaching and learning situations, and outcomes – which may be both intended and unintended – are the effects of the programme. Stake developed a matrix as part of his model (see Stake, 1967, and Jenkins, 1976, for further details) to pull together the descriptive data, and then use it to make judgements about its effects. One advantage of Stake's model and its associated matrix is that it helps distinguish between the description and judgement aspects of the evaluation. Stake uses the term *portrayal* to describe the report generated by his model of different perspectives on the programme being evaluated. His countenance model, with its use of portrayals, has parallels with illuminative evaluation in that both place a high value on description and see it as a means of gathering valuable and relevant information on a new programme from different perspectives.

Michael Scriven: goal-free evaluation

A contrasting model to that of Stake is the goal-free evaluation model developed in the USA by Michael Scriven (Scriven, 1973). Again, this model emerged from a dissatisfaction with classical research methods of evaluation, but what is distinctive about Scriven's model is that the evaluation is undertaken without reference to any statements of outcomes produced by the programme developers. This 'goal-free' approach focuses on evaluating a programme in relation to the extent to which it meets needs. The logic behind this approach, Scriven argues, is that a programme has to go beyond achieving its goals and to do something worthwhile as well. Scriven's model also differs from illuminative evaluation and Stake's portrayals in that it does not seek to establish the views of the various participants in the programme on the issues which should form the basis of the evaluation. Rather, a checklist is used to rate aspects of the programme in terms of, for example, the need for its introduction, its potential market and its cost-effectiveness. Scriven's model appears to have been less influential than that of illuminative evaluation or Stake's portrayals. Scriven was, however, the first to use the terms *summative* and *formative* to distinguish between the evaluation carried out at the end of a programme and that carried out during the programme (Scriven, 1967).

The teacher-as-researcher model

A different, but very important, model of educational evaluation is that of the teacher-as-researcher which has its origins in the work of Laurence Stenhouse in the UK. As mentioned in an earlier section, Stenhouse (1975) sees evaluation as a key element of curriculum development, with the two merging as research. Stenhouse also sees teachers as having a crucial role to play in evaluation

> . . . all well-founded curriculum research and development
> . . . is based in the study of classrooms. It thus rests on the
> work of teachers. It is not enough that teachers' work
> should be studied: they need to study it themselves. My
> theme . . . is the role of the teacher as a researcher . . .
>
> (1975, 143)

In proposing his teacher-as-researcher model, Stenhouse argues for the use of social anthropological approaches to evaluative research undertaken by teachers, drawing on observation and interpretation of lessons. The approaches Stenhouse advocates in his model therefore overlap considerably with those of illuminative evaluation, though with the teacher fulfilling the dual role of teacher and researcher/evaluator. For any teacher engaging in this task, there are issues which need to be addressed concerning potential bias and subjectivity in data which is being gathered and interpreted by someone who is a participant-observer. Nonetheless, the teacher-as-researcher (or practitioner researcher) model gained considerable ground in the 1980s and 1990s, with studies often taking the form of case studies and/or action research (i.e. research aimed at improving aspects of practice).

Evaluation and the intended, implemented *and* achieved *curriculum*

Another approach to evaluation has been to see a new programme as consisting of three main aspects: the *intended curriculum*, the *implemented curriculum* and the *achieved curriculum* (Robitaille *et al.*, 1993). This model has its origins in that developed for the International Studies of Educational Achievement (IEA studies), undertaken over a number of years in the 1970s and 1980s. The intended curriculum refers to the aims and objectives of the programme as specified by those developing the programme and the materials to support its introduction and use. The implemented curriculum concerns what happens in practice in the classroom, and the teaching approaches, learning activities and materials teachers draw on when using the programme. The implemented curriculum is very likely to differ both from the intended curriculum and from teacher to teacher, as it depends on how teachers respond to the new programme and how they interpret and choose to use its associated materials. One aspect of an evaluation is therefore to explore the extent to which the implemented curriculum matches the intended curriculum. The third aspect, the attained curriculum, relates to the outcomes of the programme: the knowledge, skills, understanding and attitudes displayed by the students who experience the programme. A second stage of evaluation is therefore to look at these aspects and relate them both to the intended and the implemented curriculum.

Ways of characterizing research and evaluation questions

As the preceding discussion has demonstrated, there are many ways in which evaluation may be characterized. One further perspective comes from work done on the sorts of questions evaluations set out to answer. Miles and Huberman (1994) provide a useful typology, categorizing evaluation questions according to whether they are *causal* (i.e. looking for links between cause and effect) or *non-causal* (i.e. seeking to gather information), and related to policy and/or management. Table 2.3 summarizes their categories of questions, with examples of each type.

The notion of causal and non-causal questions is also central to two other potentially useful classifications which have emerged in the early 2000s: that of Shavelson and Towne in the USA, and the EPPI-Centre in the UK.

Shavelson and Towne (2001) divide research studies into three broad groups. These are:

- description: seeking answers to questions about *what is happening*;
- cause: seeking answers to questions about *whether effects are systematic*;
- process or mechanism: seeking answers to questions about *why or how effects are happening*.

The Evidence for Policy and Practice Information and Co-ordinating Centre (EPPI Centre) is overseeing systematic reviews of research studies in a number of areas in education, and has proposed the following classification for studies (EPPI-Centre, 2002).

A   Description
B   Exploration of relationships
C   Evaluation (both of naturally occurring events and those which are researcher-manipulated, i.e. where the researcher introduces and evaluates a change)

Table 2.3 Typology of evaluation questions

Type of question	General forms	Sample question
Causal-research	Does X cause Y?	Do children read better as a result of this programme?
	Does X cause more of Y than Z causes of Y?	Do children read better as a result of this programme compared with another programme?
Non-causal research	What is X?	What is the daily experience of the children participating in this programme?
	Is X located where Y is lowest?	Are the remedial centres located in the areas of primary need?
Non-causal policy	What does Y mean?	What do we mean by special education children, and remediation?
	Why does S support X?	Is this programme receiving support from state and local officials for political rather than educational reasons?
Non-causal evaluation	What makes W good?	What are the characteristics of the best Computer Assisted Instruction (CAI) materials being used?
	Does T value X?	How do the various minority groups view this programme and judge its quality?
Non-causal management	Is X more cost-effective than Z?	What is the cost-effectiveness of the programme compared with other programmes?
	How are U maximized and V minimized simultaneously?	How can we maximize the scheduling of classes at the centre with the minimum of expense?

Adapted from Miles and Huberman, 1994, 24.

D   Discussion of methodology
E   Reviews

Categories B and C are of particular relevance to evaluation studies.

What is of interest in the context of educational evaluation is that both these classifications have emerged from discussion and debate about the nature of educational research and the appropriateness of experimental approaches in research and evaluation. Although the classifications cover a range of different types of study, the groups who have produced them also appear to be intimating that educational research and evaluation would benefit from including more studies of an experimental nature.

The politics of educational evaluation

Lawton's inclusion of a political model in his summary (which corresponds to Stake's management and social policy analysis approaches) points to an important aspect of educational evaluation: its political dimension. MacDonald (1976) summarizes the situation for evaluators as follows:

> Evaluators rarely see themselves as political figures, yet their work can be regarded as inherently political, and its varying styles and methods expressing different attitudes to the power distribution in education.
>
> (1976, 125)

MacDonald argues that evaluators have a responsibility which goes beyond making judgements and passing these on to decision-makers. They also need to ensure that the information they provide enables a more rational choice to be made and, in providing information, they need be aware that decision-makers will bring their own values to bear when making choices.

Although MacDonald's paper was written a number of years ago, the issues it raises about the political dimension of educational evaluation are even more pertinent in the current climate, which is characterized by much more prescription and centralized control of the curriculum, and a drive to raise standards. The politicization of educational evaluation has also been exacerbated by the moves towards what Hopkins (1989) refers to as 'categorical funding' of educational initiatives. Here, a central policy is developed, and funds made available to attract those who have the means to develop the resources needed to implement the policy. Those accepting the funds would appear to be, to a very large extent, also accepting the policy itself. As evaluation data will always be influenced by the values of those interpreting the results, any evaluation undertaken within the context of categorically funded initiatives is bound to have a strong political dimension. Moreover, changes in the structure of school education in the last decade have served only to increase this politicization of educational evaluation. (More detailed discussions of the political dimension of educational evaluation may be found in MacDonald (1976) and Norris (1990).)

Recent trends and developments in educational evaluation

In the 1970s and 1980s, the approaches advocated in the illuminative evaluation model influenced much educational evaluation. However, by the late 1980s and early 1990s, it was becoming apparent that the tide was beginning to turn, and people were looking once again at the possibilities offered by more experimental approaches to evaluation. A number of factors contributed to the raising of the profile of experimental approaches at this time. Many countries were experiencing increasingly centralized control of education in a climate of growing accountability and a drive to raise standards. Concern was also being expressed about the lack of impact of the findings of educational research and evaluation.

In the UK, a fierce debate was launched when David

Hargreaves, of the University of Cambridge, gave the annual Teacher Training Agency (TTA) lecture in 1996 (Hargreaves, 1996). He argued that schools would be more effective if teaching became a research-based profession, and blamed researchers for supposedly failing to make this happen. Hargreaves also accused researchers of producing 'inconclusive and contestable findings of little worth', and went on to say

> . . . just how much research is there which (i) demonstrates conclusively that if teachers change their practice from x to y there will be a significant and enduring improvement in teaching and learning, and (ii) has developed an effective method of convincing teachers of the benefits of, and means to, changing from x to y?
>
> (1996, 5)

Hargreaves was not alone in his criticism, and many of the points he made were echoed in other documents, such as the reports of two subsequent inquiries into educational research (Tooley and Darbey, 1998; Hillage *et al.*, 1998). Underpinning all these critiques was the notion that much educational research is 'unscientific', because it fails to draw on the experimental techniques of the natural sciences. As such, it also fails to 'deliver the goods' in terms of making recommendations for practice which can be implemented with confidence.

In his lecture, Hargreaves encouraged the educational research community to look to medical research and the approaches adopted in evidence-based medicine as a good model for research whose procedures supposedly allowed definite conclusions to be reached about what works. In evidence-based medicine, controlled trials of particular treatments are undertaken to establish if they work. Hargreaves argued that educational research should follow a similar approach – evidence-based education.

Randomized controlled trials

A key technique in evidence-based medicine is that of the randomized controlled trial (RCT). Oakley (2000) describes RCTs as follows:

> An RCT is simply an experiment ('trial') which tests alternative ways of handling a situation. Sometimes the intervention is tested against what would have happened had it not been used; sometimes different interventions are compared.

> (2000, 18)

A key aspect of an RCT is that, although members are allocated randomly to groups, the groups being compared are as similar in composition as possible. Thus, in medical trials of a particular treatment, groups might contain similar distributions of people in terms of, for example, age, sex and social class. In order to achieve similarity in group composition, and to ensure findings are reliable and valid, RCTs require large sample groups.

In the late 1990s and early 2000s, a number of people are advocating the use of RCTs in educational research and evaluation (for example Boruch, 1997; Fitz-Gibbon, 2000; Torgerson and Torgerson, 2001). The technique is seen as a way of enabling claims about cause and effect to be made with more confidence than has formerly been the case in educational research and evaluation. Although RCTs purport to yield conclusive results about what does and does not work, they need to be treated with caution in educational research and evaluation. As Millar (2002) has pointed out, there are some key differences between medical 'treatments' and educational 'treatments' in terms of what they set out to do. A medical treatment is normally undertaken to restore a desired state of normality; an educational programme is usually developed in order to achieve different outcomes to current programmes. Thus it is not possible to make direct comparisons between the programmes in the way that an RCT seeks to do.

Interest in RCTs is not confined to the UK. Their potential utility has been debated extensively in the USA, where there is a stronger tradition of experimental research. One outcome of the debate was that the National Research Council in the USA set up a panel to consider and advise on approaches to educational research and evaluation. The subsequent report, 'Scientific Enquiry in Education' (Shavelson and Towne, 2001), considers the merits of a number of approaches to research and evaluation, as summarized earlier in this section. They conclude that RCTs may have a useful role in some situations, but other approaches which generate more descriptive and explanatory findings also have an important part to play in educational research and evaluation.

Much of the current debate about the potential utility of RCTs is reminiscent of that which took place in the 1970s on the limitations of the classical research model in educational evaluation. A key question with RCTs concerns when such a technique is appropriate, and it will be interesting to see in the next few years the extent of the impact of RCTs on the evaluation of new educational programmes.

Design experiments

Another comparatively recent development in educational evaluation is the *design experiment*. The term has its origins in the work of Ann Brown (Brown, 1992) and Allan Collins (Collins, 1993) in the USA. Design experiments draw on the evaluation approaches used in technology and engineering, which aim to explore how a product, developed to solve a particular problem, performs in selected situations. This has clear parallels in educational contexts, where the 'product' being tested is a new programme, developed with the intention of addressing selected problems or shortcomings within the existing system.

A design experiment in educational contexts involves evaluating the effects of a new programme in a limited number of settings. For example, this might involve selecting teachers who teach roughly comparable groups, but who have different teaching styles, and exploring the effects of the new programme on each group of students. The design experiment would then yield information on the circumstances in which the programme is likely to be most successful. Design experiments see the context in which the programme is introduced as an important factor likely to influence its success, and also acknowledge that those implementing the programme are highly likely to make modifications in order to tailor it to their own particular situations. Thus, there may be considerable variation in what happens in practice from one context to another.

Design experiments have features in common with both illuminative evaluation and the classical research approach to evaluation. They resemble the former in seeking to describe and explain what happens in selected settings. However, within this they also seek to test out particular hypotheses, and as such incorporate a dimension of the classical approach.

As with RCTs, the impact of design experiments in educational evaluation is yet to be seen. Where they seem to have particular advantages is in their ability to encompass the complexity of educational settings and interactions, whilst also enabling the aims of new educational programmes to be tested systematically. As such, they appear to offer a potentially fruitful approach to evaluation which is sympathetic to the nature and purpose of many new educational programmes.

Summary

This section has provided an overview of different perspectives on the models and approaches associated with educational evaluation. In particular, it has shown that

- several different models of evaluation have been developed, some of which bring very different perspectives to bear on the process of evaluation;
- the two most contrasting models are provided by the classical research model and illuminative evaluation;

- both the classical research model and illuminative evaluation have their adherents and critics;
- evaluation questions can be characterized in a number of ways, with some simply wanting to know 'what works?', and others wanting to know 'how is it working?' or 'why is it working in this particular way?';
- there is a political dimension to educational evaluation;
- recent moves to encourage the educational research community to look to the approaches adopted in medical research have resulted in an increased interest in the classical research model in the form of Randomized Controlled Trials (RCTs).

3

Curriculum Innovation and Models of Change

This section looks at models of change which have been developed from examining the effects of curriculum innovation and the implications of such models for evaluation.

Introduction

In the previous section, a number of models and approaches to educational evaluation were discussed, which point to issues needing to be taken into consideration when planning and designing an evaluation. These models are complemented by others which have been developed to describe the effects of programme implementation. The two models described in this section are the *Concerns-Based Adoption Model* (*CBAM*) developed in the USA, and the *typology of continuing professional development* (*CPD*) *outcomes* developed in the UK. These two models have been selected for a number of reasons. Both are empirically-based and have been developed from detailed studies of the effects of introducing new programmes in a range of different contexts. Both have also sought to identify the factors which seem to contribute to the success – or otherwise – of an innovation. As such, they have a direct bearing on educational evaluation because they help provide answers to questions about how and why a new programme is – or is not – working. The models differ in that the CBAM model places its emphasis on the process of change which accompanies the introduction

42

of a new programme, whereas the typology of CPD outcomes, as its name suggests, focuses on the effects or outcomes of in-service work provided to support the implementation of a new programme.

The models draw on the work of a number of others who have undertaken detailed studies of curriculum innovation and its effects, most notably that of Michael Fullan in Canada and Bruce Joyce and Beverley Showers in the United States. Their work is summarized briefly here in order to provide context for the two models described in this section.

One of Fullan's key publications is *The Meaning of Educational Change* (Fullan, 1982, third edition, 2001). Fullan argues that there are three dimensions at stake in implementing a new programme:

- the possible use of new or revised materials;
- the possible use of new teaching approaches;
- the possible alteration of beliefs (2001, p39).

He suggests that change is composed of four phases: initiation, implementation, continuation and outcome. In educational contexts, *initiation* involves the processes leading up to the decision to adopt a new programme, *implementation* involves the first experiences of using the new programme, *continuation* refers to the time when the programme is either integrated into the system or discarded, and *outcome* is the degree of improvement in, for example, students' learning and attitudes, teacher satisfaction, and overall school improvement. Fullan argues that the lack of success of many innovations can be attributed to the failure of policy-makers, curriculum developers and those implementing the innovation to understand the process of change.

Bruce Joyce and Beverley Showers have focused on staff development as a key element of successful change. In their earlier work, they suggest that there are four categories of levels of impact in in-service training:

- awareness;
- the acquisition of concepts or organized knowledge;

- the learning of principles and skills;
- the ability to apply those principles and skills in the class-room (1980, 380).

Their more recent work (Joyce and Showers, 1995) has identi-fied a number of key components which are necessary for effective in-service training. These include:

- describing new skills to teachers through, for example, talks and lectures;
- demonstrating new skills and techniques to teachers;
- providing opportunities for teachers to develop and practice these skills and techniques in simulated and real settings;
- giving teachers feedback on performance;
- coaching teachers on the job.

Joyce and Showers place particular emphasis on this last aspect – which they term *peer coaching* – as a central element of effective in-service training.

The Concerns-Based Adoption Model (CBAM)

The Concerns-Based Adoption Model (CBAM) was developed over a number of years by a team at the University of Texas at Austin in the USA. The team was concerned that many new programmes introduced into schools appeared to meet with little success and were often discarded, a situation which is certainly not unique to the USA. This led to a detailed study of the process of change in schools and classrooms covering the introduction of a range of different programmes. The initial work was undertaken by Hall *et al.*, (1973), and is described in detail in Shirley Hord's book, *Evaluating Educational Innovation* (Hord, 1987), a book written with classroom practitioners as its principal audience. Hord summarizes the CBAM model as follows:

> The Concerns-Based Adoption Model is an empirically-based conceptual framework which outlines the develop-

mental process that individuals experience as they implement an innovation.

(1987, 93)

She goes on to suggest that there are three general questions about an innovation that the model can help to answer:

- What would I like to see happen with the innovation?
- How can I make that happen?
- How is it going?

The model is based on seven basic assumptions about change:

1 Change is a process, not an event.
2 Change is made by individuals first.
3 Change is a highly personal experience.
4 Change entails multi-level developmental growth (i.e. it will involve shifts in feelings, skills and behaviours).
5 Change is best understood in operational terms (i.e. teachers who have to implement the change need to be able to relate it readily to what it means for their classroom practice).
6 Change facilitation must suit individual needs (i.e. it must address the concerns and problems of those implementing the change).
7 Change efforts should focus on individuals, not innovations (i.e. the innovation needs to be seen as extending beyond the materials it produces to the role of the individuals who will use the materials).

The CBAM model has four components. The first relates to how teachers feel about an innovation, the second to how they use it, the third to what the innovation means in practice as a result of it being used, and the fourth to implementing strategies to aid the change process.

A cornerstone of the CBAM model is a seven-level description of *Stages of Concern*, which identifies teachers' feelings in relation to an innovation. This is summarized in Table 3.1.

The lowest level of concern in the CBAM model is Stage 0, where an individual has little or no awareness of an innovation and it is therefore not of concern to them. There then follow three stages where those implementing the change are predominantly focused on their own thoughts and needs. At Stage 1, an individual realizes that an innovation exists, and wants to know more about it. Stage 2 is characterized by intense personal concern about new demands and expectation, with questions such as 'What does it mean for me?' and 'How is it going to affect me?' being asked. As the individual begins to use the innovation, they will reach Stage 3, where basic concerns over management (time, logistics, paperwork) predominate. Hord argues that a failure to acknowledge the support that individuals need at this stage is likely to lead to an innovation being unsuccessful. If, however, individuals become sufficiently comfortable and confident with managerial aspects, they then move to Stage 4 of the model and away from self-focused concerns towards consideration of the consequences of the innovation for their students. By Stage 5, teachers want to share their ideas and collaborate with others using the same innovation in order to maximize the benefit for their students from the innovation. Finally, in Stage 6, teachers want to modify the innovation for themselves to improve their practice still further.

Table 3.1 The stages of concern in the Concerns-Based Adoption Model (CBAM)

Stages of concern	Expressions of concern
6 Refocusing	I have some ideas about something that would work even better
5 Collaboration	I am concerned about relating what I am doing with what other instructors are doing
4 Consequence	How is my use affecting students?
3 Management	I seem to be spending all my time getting materials ready
2 Personal	How will using it affect me?
1 Informational	I would like to know more about it
0 Awareness	I am not concerned about it (the innovation)

Taken from Hord, 1987, 101.

Hord suggests that gathering information during an innovation is essential. This can be done by asking individuals to complete open-ended statements, or by conducting interviews. (The CBAM team has also developed a copyright-protected written questionnaire, the '*Stages of Concern Questionnaire*' (Hall *et al.*, 1973), which enables identification of the stage a teacher has reached. The questionnaire and accompanying manual are available for purchase.)

Although teachers' feelings about an innovation are highly likely to influence its effects, what matters in practice is what teachers actually do – the behaviours and skills they demonstrate in relation to an innovation. The CBAM model therefore supplements the seven stages of concern with descriptions of eight levels of use. These are summarized in Table 3.2.

Levels 0, I and II are associated with non-users, although Levels I and II indicate some involvement, first through activities such as attending workshops and discussions with users and then through gathering together the resources needed to implement the innovation. Levels III onward describe behaviours of users. At Level III, the individual is preoccupied with logistical concerns such as getting organized and preparing materials. Hord's work suggests that many individuals remain at this stage for a long time, and may never get beyond it without training and support. Level IVA corresponds to a 'breathing space', where the immediate stresses and strains associated with implementation have passed. At Level IVB and higher, the user moves beyond basic survival and routine use to behaviours focusing directly on improving the student experience.

Hord suggest that interviews are the most appropriate way of gathering data on levels of use. However, these would appear to run the risk of merely gathering information on reported behaviour, rather than actual behaviour. Supplementing interview data with observation would seem to be essential in gathering valid data on levels of use.

The final strand of the CBAM model focuses on the innovation itself, and what is actually happening when it is being

Table 3.2 The Levels of Use in the Concerns-Based Adoption Model (CBAM)

Level of use	Behavioural indices of Level
VI Renewal	The user is seeking more effective alternatives to the established use of the innovation
V Integration	The user is making deliberate efforts to coordinate with others in using the innovation
IVB Refinement	The user is making changes to increase outcomes
IVA Routine	The user is making few or no changes and has an established pattern of use
III Mechanical use	The user is making changes to organize better use of the innovation
II Preparation	I would like to know more about it
I Orientation	The individual is seeking information about the innovation
0 Non-use	No action is being taken with respect to the innovation

Taken from Hord, 1987, 111.

used. As Hord comments, no two teachers will use an innovation in exactly the same way, but will integrate it in some way with their existing practice. Therefore, judgements about the effectiveness of an innovation need to be set in the context of what the innovation means in practice. The CBAM model terms this the *Innovation Configuration*. In order to find out what is happening, Hord recommends interviewing key people associated with an innovation. These are the developers, and those she terms the *change facilitators*: the people providing the training and support for the innovation, who may or may not be the developers. She suggests three key questions should be asked:

- What would you hope to observe when the innovation is operational?
- What would teachers and others be doing?
- What are the critical components of the innovation?

This is then followed by interviews with a small number of users, and observation of their lessons to check on the user's views of the innovation and what is happening in practice. Based on these interviews and observations, a checklist based on the key components is produced. This can contain items relating to, for example, the teacher's use of the materials, how lessons are structured, record-keeping, and assessment. The checklist can then be completed through observation of a wider sample of users.

Armed with information about stages of concern, levels of use and innovation configurations, the developers and trainers (change facilitators) can then put together a programme of interventions to support the innovation. Such a programme might include in-service provision, setting up support networks and providing consultation on an individual basis.

A number of messages about innovation have emerged from Hord's work with the CBAM model. Key factors which have been shown to contribute to the success of an innovation are long-term planning, allowing sufficient time for an innovation to become accepted and used, and supporting teachers through in-service provision before and during implementation.

One strength of the CBAM model is that anyone who has been involved in the implementation of a new programme can almost always readily identify many or all of the stages of concern and levels of use described. A further strength lies in its flexibility: it can be applied to innovations of different scales, tailored to fit different needs and expectations, and it allows data to be gathered which can inform both summative and formative evaluation.

John Harland and Kay Kinder: a typology of continuing professional development (CPD) outcomes

The model developed by Harland and Kinder emerged from a specific concern about the outcomes and effects of in-service training (INSET) and continuing professional development (CPD) in the UK. As many – although by no means all – new programmes which are introduced are accompanied by some form of training for teachers, exploring the impact of such training sheds light on factors which may contribute to the level of the programme's subsequent success.

Harland and Kinder felt that research into the implementation of new programmes had emphasized the process at the expense of looking at the outcomes, although, as they acknowledge

> Ultimately, of course, any comprehensive theory of INSET must take account of both an empirically-validated model of outcomes and its relationship to the processes associated with the many different forms of CPD provision and activity.
>
> (1997, 72)

The development of their model resulted from work on a study of a staff development programme for the introduction of science into primary schools (Kinder and Harland, 1991) following the introduction of the National Curriculum in England and Wales (DES/WO, 1989), which made science a compulsory subject in primary schools. The data on which the model is based were gathered in five case-study schools over a period of four years, through detailed observation and interviews with key personnel.

Harland and Kinder proposed a typology of nine INSET outcomes, which they suggest, show how existing models of in-service training, such as those of Fullan and Joyce and Showers, could be enhanced. Their typology is summarized in Table 3.3.

Harland and Kinder's research suggests that *material and provisionary outcomes*, or the physical resources made available to teachers, can have a very positive effect on practice. However, their work also indicates that these alone are unlikely to have much effect, unless accompanied by *motivational outcomes* and *new knowledge and skills* (see below). They also contrast their model with Fullan's model of change (Fullan, 1991). The latter model has *initiation* as the first phase, involving acquisition and use of new materials. Harland and Kinder suggest that it is useful to separate these two aspects, as it is possible for teachers to acquire new materials but not use them, and changes in

Table 3.3 A typology of in-service training (INSET) outcomes

Outcome	Definition
1 Material and provisionary outcomes	The physical resources which result from participation in INSET activities
2 Informational outcomes	The state of being briefed or cognisant of background facts and news about curriculum management developments, including their implications for practice
3 New awareness	Perceptual or conceptual shift from previous assumptions of what constitutes appropriate content and delivery of a particular curriculum area
4 Value congruence outcomes	The personalized versions of curriculum and classroom management which inform a practitioner's teaching, and how far these 'individual codes of practice' come to coincide with INSET messages about 'good practice'
5 Affective outcomes	The emotional experience inherent in any learning situation
6 Motivational and attitudinal outcomes	Enhanced enthusiasm and motivation to implement the ideas received during INSET experiences
7 Knowledge and skills	Deeper levels of understanding critical reflexivity and theoretical outcomes, with regard to both curriculum content and the teaching/learning process
8 Institutional outcomes	Collective impact on groups of teachers and their practice
9 Impact on practice	The ultimate intention to bring about changes in practice

Adapted from Kinder *et al.*, 1991, 57–8.

practice can be severely impeded if teachers do not have the necessary resources to support the changes.

Harland and Kinder have also identified two linked sets of outcomes: *informational outcomes* and *new knowledge and skills*. The former simply refers to teachers being briefed about the background and facts relating to the innovation, including management and implications for practice whereas the latter applies to a deeper and more critical understanding of the curriculum content and teaching approaches. Harland and Kinder's work suggests that this deeper understanding is one of the essential requirements for the success of an innovation.

Two further linked outcomes are *new awareness* and *value congruence*. *New awareness* is a term often used by teachers themselves, and describes a shift from previous assumptions about appropriate curriculum content and delivery. However, Harland and Kinder's work suggests that new awareness alone is insufficient to bring about change. For this to happen, there also needs to be *value congruence*, or significant overlap between a teacher's individual code of practice and the messages given by the in-service training about what constitutes 'good practice'. Value congruence outcomes, as with new knowledge and skills, emerged as crucial to the success of an innovation.

The typology also makes provision for the emotional responses that will inevitably be associated with any innovation. This is done through *affective outcomes* and *motivational and attitudinal outcomes*. *Affective outcomes* refer to teachers' initial responses to the in-service training. Where these are negative, perhaps as a result of teachers feeling demoralized by their experiences in the in-service provision, the innovation is unlikely to be successful. Even initially positive responses may not lead to success if teachers do not also gain the associated new knowledge and skills needed to support their teaching. *Motivational and attitudinal outcomes* refer to the enhanced enthusiasm and motivation to implement the work that teachers gain through their experiences of the in-service provision. Harland and Kinder established that affective outcomes were important precursors for impact on practice.

The final set of outcomes in the typology are *institutional outcomes*. These recognize that in-service work can have a collective impact on groups of teachers and their practice, with collaboration and mutual support contributing to the success of the innovation.

Harland and Kinder's work led them to conclude that the

presence of certain outcomes was more likely to achieve developments in practice than others. Thus, they proposed a hierarchy of INSET outcomes (see Table 3.4).

Harland and Kinder suggest that in-service experiences which offer – or are perceived to offer – only third order outcomes, i.e. those which raise awareness and provide materials and information, are unlikely to have an impact on practice unless some of the other outcomes are already present. The second order outcomes, including motivational and affective outcomes, were important in contributing to success, but substantial impact on practice was consistently associated with the presence of the two first order outcomes: value congruence, and new knowledge and skills. In reaching this conclusion, Harland and Kinder also note that other outcomes are likely to be present if these two first order outcomes are present, and that successful implementation requires all the outcomes, as prioritized in the hierarchy, to be either achieved through the in-service provision or present as pre-existing conditions.

The Harland and Kinder typology of CPD outcomes shares the same advantages of the CBAM model in that it 'rings true' to anyone who has been involved with in-service training. As with the CBAM model, it also lends itself to adaptation for a variety of different circumstances.

Table 3.4   A hierarchy of in-service training (INSET) outcomes

	INSET input		
3rd order	Provisionary	Information	New awareness
2nd order	Motivation	Affective	Institutional
1st order	Value congruence	Knowledge and skills	
	Impact on practice		

Taken from Harland and Kinder, 1997, 77.

Summary

This section has provided an overview of two different models of change, one focusing on the process of change and the other on the outcomes of in-service provision aimed at supporting change. These models have suggested that

- change is a complex process which involves several stages;
- support is needed for those implementing a new programme to help them move from one stage to another;
- certain factors are crucial to the success of a new programme, such as the extent to which the aims of the programme fit with teachers' views of what constitutes good practice;
- studies of the process of change point to areas which should be explored in an evaluation in order to answer questions about *how* and *why* a new programme is working in particular ways.

4

Research Strategies and Techniques for Educational Evaluation

This section has two main aims:

- to provide a brief overview of the most common research strategies and techniques employed in educational evaluation;
- to consider the benefits of using a multi-method approach to educational evaluation.

Research strategies and techniques

This section provides a very brief overview of the research strategies and techniques commonly employed in evaluation. Details of sources of further information may be found in the Appendix.

Educational evaluation draws on the research strategies and techniques of the sciences and social sciences. There are five main strategies used in educational research: action research, case study, ethnography, experiment, and survey. Of these strategies, evaluation commonly employs experiments and case studies. Where the evaluation is gathering data on a large-scale programme in a number of locations, the strategy could also be described as a survey. Evaluation is also linked to action research, in that one dimension of action research involves practitioner-researchers evaluating the effects of changes they have made in their own practice. Table 4.1 summarizes the key characteristics of experiments and case studies.

Table 4.1 Characteristics of experiments and case studies

	Experiment	*Case study*
Purpose	To test a hypothesis	To examine an educational practice in a specific instance
Advantages	Can provide strong evidence linking particular factors to particular outcomes	Can reveals subtleties and intricacies of situations and explanations for outcomes
Disadvantages	• Matching of control and experimental groups can be difficult • Focuses on outcomes not process, therefore does not yield information or answer how or why particular outcomes arise	The extent to which results are generalizable
Other points	• Normally associated with summative evaluation and quantitative data • Requires sample sizes of at least 30 for random allocation into control and experimental groups	• Often associated with formative evaluation and qualitative data, though may also make use of some quantitative data • Often draws on more than one research technique

A range of research techniques for data collection is available to educational evaluators. The five most commonly used are document study, focus groups, interviews, observation, and questionnaires, although a number of other techniques can also be employed. Table 4.2 summarizes the key characteristics of these techniques.

Decisions about research strategies and techniques are closely linked to the overall purpose of an evaluation and whether it will have a summative or formative emphasis. These decisions usually carry with them implications for the strategy or strategies to be followed, which, in turn, point to particular research techniques and emphasize particular types of data.

Other research techniques

A number of other research techniques may be useful in an evaluation to supplement data gathered through the main techniques described above. These include audio and video recordings, photographs, field notes (i.e. notes made by the evaluator) and participant diaries (i.e. records and notes made by those participating in the evaluation).

The case for a multi-method approach

A central aim of any evaluation is to provide the best possible information which can be collected within the constraints on the study. However, as the first part of this book has demonstrated, there is no consensus over what data should be gathered in an evaluation study, or how it should be gathered. Equally, the information in this section has served to illustrate that each of the research strategies and techniques has its associated advantages and disadvantages. These factors point very strongly to the value of employing a *multi-method approach* in educational evaluation: in other words, an approach which contains both formative and summative dimensions, which draws on a range of research strategies and techniques, and which generates both qualitative and quantitative data.

Multi-method approaches have a number of associated benefits:

- they permit exploration of both the outcomes and processes associated with a new programme;
- they result in improved and enriched findings, yielding greater understanding of what is happening, why it is happening and how it is happening;
- they permit modifications to be made to aspects of the

Table 4.2 Key characteristics of research techniques used in evaluation

Technique	Useful for data on . . .	Advantages	Disadvantages
Document study (e.g. policy statements, handbooks, annual reports minutes of meetings, transcripts of students' work, test results, institution databases)	• National and local background to the introduction of a new programme • The context into which a new programme is being introduced • Existing data on students' performance in tests and examinations	• Provides a picture of the institution(s) in terms of its culture, priorities, values, resources and performance • Materials are generally readily available (though access may need to be negotiated)	• Time needed to read the documents • Possible difficulties with developing frameworks for the analysis of very diverse sources of data
Focus group	• Identifying problems during programme implementation • Identifying the strengths and weaknesses of a programme	• Comparatively quick probing of views	• Time requirements for conducting, transcribing and analysing data
Interview	• Participants' knowledge about a programme and their expectations of it • The experiences, views and motives of participants in a programme • How teachers are coping with a new programme and identifying areas where support is needed	• Rich data and insights • Face-to-face contact with participants in the programme • Allow the evaluator to clarify and probe responses • Permit flexibility if unexpected areas emerge	• Time requirements for conducting, transcribing and analysing data (with likely cost implications) • The large volume of data which may be gathered

Observation	• The context of a setting • Behaviours and actions of participants, including verbal and non-verbal interactions • What is actually happening when a new programme is introduced	• Provides a picture of the context in which a programme is being implemented • Can yield information on unexpected outcomes or aspects of which participants are unaware	• Time requirements for gathering and analysing data • The impact on the participants of having an observer present • Elements of observer bias in selecting the data to be recorded
Questionnaire	• Teachers' views of a programme • Teachers' reported behaviours in relation to a programme (which can be verified from observation data) • Students' views on particular aspects of their experience	• An efficient use of time for both evaluator and respondent • Standardization of questions • The possibility of respondent anonymity, which may lead to more candid and honest responses • Data analysis is normally straightforward and not overly time-consuming	• Difficult to explore issues in depth • Respondents can only answer the questions they are asked, therefore unanticipated issues will not emerge • 'Questionnaire overload' – many people receive a lot of questionnaires and may therefore be inclined to answer them quickly and superficially, if at all

evaluation plan should unanticipated outcomes worthy of further exploration be encountered;

- they generate multiple sources of data which provide checks on the validity and trustworthiness of the findings.

Summary

This section has outlined the main types of data collected in evaluation studies, and the principal strategies and techniques employed. In particular, it has shown that:

- evaluation studies can collect quantitative and qualitative data;
- evaluation studies in education are normally associated with experimental research strategies or case studies, each of which has its advantages and disadvantages;
- a variety of techniques is employed to gather evaluation data, including document studies, questionnaires, observation, interviews and focus groups;
- effective and informative educational evaluation is likely to involve a range of techniques and to gather a variety of data, i.e. it uses a multi-method approach.

5

Planning and Doing
an Evaluation

This section explores ways in which the ideas covered above can be applied to the planning and undertaking of an evaluation.

Key questions when planning and undertaking an evaluation

A number of questions need to be addressed when planning and undertaking an evaluation. These are summarized in Box 5.1. A first point to make about these questions is that they point to a number of theoretical and practical issues which need to be

---

Box 5.1   Key questions when planning an evaluation

- What is being evaluated?
- What form will the evaluation take?
- What practical issues (time, money, staff skills, timescale) need to be taken into account?
- What questions will the evaluation address?
- What use will be made of the findings?
- What types of data will be collected to help answer the evaluation questions?
- What techniques will be used to gather the data?
- Who will gather the data?
- What ethical considerations need to be addressed?
- How will the evaluation be reported?

---

resolved in planning an evaluation. Earlier sections have given some indication of the areas of debate about theoretical issues, which generally focus on the value of different approaches to evaluation and the nature and purpose of the data collected. Practical issues concern matters such as time and constraints, and the skills and abilities of those undertaking the evaluation.

A second point to make about the questions is that they do not form a 'recipe' to be followed step by step. In some cases, particularly where they relate to theoretical considerations, answering one question in a particular way will influence responses to others. Moreover, there are many ways of undertaking educational evaluation, and no formula exists which can be applied and guaranteed to work in all situations.

An important initial step in an evaluation study is the production of a plan. This sets the agenda for the evaluation, specifies the questions to be asked and the ways in which information will be gathered to help answer them, and gives a timescale for the work. In a large-scale evaluation, the plan may well form the basis of a contract. The process of answering the questions in Box 5.1 will help with the production of the evaluation plan.

Each of the questions in Box 5.1 is now considered in more detail. To illustrate how design principles for an evaluation may be put into practice, a hypothetical innovation (albeit one based on an actual example) is described in Box 5.2. This concerns the introduction of a support programme aimed at assisting underachieving students. Aspects of this example are used to illustrate the decision-making process in designing and undertaking an evaluation.

What is being evaluated?

In order to produce an evaluation plan, it is important to be able to describe the new programme clearly to aid identification of the aspects which are to be evaluated. Box 5.3 provides a template for producing a concise description of an evaluation,

Box 5.2   An evaluation of a support programme for underachieving students

You are a teacher and member of the senior management team in a high school which hopes to improve its overall performance in national tests and examinations. Current assessment data has revealed that the picture within the school reflects the national picture, which is one where girls are out-performing boys in tests and examinations in most subjects and at most levels. As a result, your school is working in collaboration with three other local schools to introduce a programme aimed at providing support for students aged 11 and 12. The particular target group is that of underachieving boys. This programme takes the form of monthly reviews in which underachieving students are offered advice and support in planning their work, and targets are set and reviewed. Progress is recorded in a 'Progress diary' which students are expected to show to their parents. In addition, a database of information on all students has been set up to record test and examination marks across all subjects.

The schools involved in the programme want to gather some systematic data on its effects, and you have been asked to produce a report evaluating the programme.

Box 5.3   Template for producing a description of the programme to be evaluated

- The programme is addressing the area of . . .
- The aims of the programme are . . .
- The ideas or theories underpinning the programme are . . .
- The programme takes the form of . . .
- The target groups for the programme are . . .
- The key groups of people (stakeholders) involved in the programme are . . .
- The support being provided during the programme takes the form of . . .
- Other aspects worth noting are . . .

and Box 5.4 illustrates how this might be completed for the example evaluation.

It should be noted that this template (and the others included in Section 5) are provided as a general framework for structuring thinking about aspects of an evaluation. They are not intended as a checklist to be followed mechanically, and will need to be tailored to individual circumstances.

What form will the evaluation take?

An evaluation is often characterized by its main purpose and its overall strategy. As discussed in Section 1, a key distinction often made in evaluation studies is that of *summative* and *formative* evaluation. A *summative evaluation* aims to gather data about links between the intended curriculum and the achieved curriculum. In general terms, a summative evaluation addresses questions such as:

- How successful was the programme in achieving its goals?
- How effective was the programme for different groups of participants?
- Which aspects of the programme were the most effective?

A *formative evaluation* seeks answers to questions about the process of implementation and how this relates to the achieved curriculum. Thus the main questions addressed will be:

- How does what is happening in classrooms match the goals of the programme?
- Which aspects of the programme appear to be most effective in helping those involved meet the goals of the programme and why?
- What barriers are being encountered in implementing the programme, and what strategies are being used to overcome these?

Any evaluation is likely to be strengthened if it includes both summative and formative aspects.

Box 5.4 Using the template to describe the support programme for underachieving students

- The programme is addressing the area of the differential achievement of girls and boys.
- The aims of the programme are to offer support to 11- and 12-year-old students identified as underachieving.
- No specific theory underpins the programme, although the materials which have been developed draw on research into gender issues and underachievement.
- The programme takes the form of monthly 20-minute tutorial reviews with students. A team of four teachers, one from each school, has produced a series of briefing sheets for staff to use at these tutorial reviews, and a 'Progress diary' in which students record selected information.
- The target group for the programme is students aged 11 and 12 in four schools.
- The key stakeholders are the senior management team in the schools, the teachers involved in the programme, the students involved in the programme, and the parents of the students. Additionally, the schools' administrative staff are involved in the setting up and maintaining of the database.
- Support provided takes the form of fortnightly 'twilight' sessions for staff.

An evaluation may also be characterized by the overall research strategy adopted. Traditionally, in educational evaluation, the two most common strategies are experiments and case studies, with each being linked to particular approaches to evaluation. These strategies have been described in detail in Section 4.

In the example evaluation . . .

In the case of the example evaluation of the support programme for underachieving students, a summative evaluation might well be undertaken after the programme had been

65

running for one or two years, and focus on changes in students' performance in tests and examinations. A formative evaluation would gather data during the implementation of the programme and might explore teachers' and students' opinions of the effectiveness of the programme with a view to modifying resources and improving the training and support offered to teachers to help them with the programme. It is likely that the evaluation will want to have both summative and formative dimensions. The scale of the new programme means that the evaluation will take the form of a collection of case studies, although the possibility of comparing effects across locations might also enable it to be characterized as a design experiment.

What practical issues need to be taken into account?

A number of practical issues will need to be taken into account when planning an evaluation. These are likely to include:

- the timescale for the evaluation;
- the time available for the work;
- the money available for the work;
- the level of staffing allocated to the work;
- the research skills of the staff;
- the availability and accessibility of sources of data.

Timescales may be imposed or dictated by circumstances, or there may be some flexibility. However, the timescale will certainly influence decisions about the nature and scope of the data to be collected. For example, a short timescale is likely to preclude extensive use of interviews, or other techniques which place heavy demands on time for the collection of data and the analysis of the large quantities of qualitative data likely to be gathered. A short timescale may also limit the amount of formative evaluation data which can be collected.

In addition to time demands, qualitative data collection techniques, such as interviews and focus groups, require particular skills in order to probe responses appropriately when data are being gathered. In contrast, data collection and analysis via a questionnaire is likely to be less time-consuming, although this method requires particular skills in designing the instrument and may well need some knowledge of appropriate statistical tests for data analysis.

An evaluation also has to take into account the availability and accessibility of sources of data. Whilst, for example, it might be desirable to interview all the teachers using a new programme, time and distance may well make this difficult for a large-scale programme.

In the example evaluation . . .

In the example evaluation of the support programme for underachieving students, which involves an evaluation carried out by a single researcher, the practical issues most likely to influence the design of the evaluation relate to the time made available to the researcher and the timescale for the work. A short timescale of, say, a few months and limited time would mean the evaluation was likely to draw mainly on question-naire data gathered from staff and students, followed up with a small number of interviews. Additionally, it would be possible to include only limited data on students' performance. A longer timescale of one to two years, with more time available, would permit more extensive use of interviews and a more detailed analysis of trends and patterns in students' performance in tests and examinations. A single teacher undertaking an evaluation would also have to work round constraints on access to teachers and students in other schools, who are likely to be spending the majority of their time in lessons.

What questions will the evaluation address?

The development of specific evaluation questions involves several steps:

- identifying and clarifying the goals of the new programme;
- identifying the key people involved (the 'stakeholders') and the questions likely to be of interest to them;
- identifying the audiences for the evaluation and the questions likely to be of interest to them;
- making decisions about which of the possible questions can be realistically addressed in the context of the main purposes of the evaluation and in relation to practical constraints.

Identifying and clarifying goals

A considerable investment of time and effort is often needed to identify and clarify goals. New programmes often have a number of goals, and these may be stated in very general or global terms. A key aspect of developing specific evaluation questions is to relate them to precise goals. Precise goals are those which point clearly to sources of information which will provide evidence to help answer the evaluation questions. Thus, a first step often involves the refining of stated goals to break them down into smaller and more precise goals.

Box 5.5 provides a template for identifying the goals of a new programme, and Box 5.6 illustrates how this template might be used to start identifying aspects and questions to

---

Box 5.5   Template for identifying aspects to include in an evaluation

- The goals of the programme are . . .

For each of these goals in turn:
- [If necessary] More precise components of this goal are . . .

For each of these components/goals:
- Evidence that this goal is being achieved will come from . . .
- Factors likely to influence the extent to which this goal is achieved are . . .
- The questions that need to be asked in relation to this goal are therefore . . .

Box 5.6   Using the template to start identifying aspects to include in the evaluation of the support programme for underachieving students

The specific goals of the programme are:

1   to assist underachieving students with planning and reviewing their work;
2   to develop a series of briefing sheets for staff to use with underachieving students;
3   to set up a database to monitor students' progress across all their subjects;
4   to improve the performance of underachieving students.

Goal 1

This main goal can be broken down into the following goals:

(a) to help students develop a work diary, the 'Progress diary', in which they record work set, due dates and marks, together with test and examination marks;
(b) to help students set appropriate targets for their work, and review their progress in relation to these targets.

Evidence that Goal 1(a) is being achieved will come from material in students' 'Progress Diaries'.

Factors likely to influence the extent to which Goal 1(a) is being achieved will include the extent to which staff offer guidance on what to put in the 'Progress diary', the ease of use of the diary and the time needed to complete it.

The questions that need to be asked in relation to Goal 1(a) are therefore:

• What help do staff give students in completing their 'Progress diary'?
• How easy do staff and students find the 'Progress diary' to use?
• How long does it take to complete the 'Progress diary'?
• What improvements would staff and students suggest for future versions of the 'Progress diary'?

include in the evaluation of the support programme for under-achieving students.

Identifying stakeholders and audiences

In addition to those exploring aspects of the goals of a new programme, evaluation questions also emerge from the needs, experiences and priorities of the key people involved in the programme (the 'stakeholders'), and the priorities and interests of those reading the evaluation report. Depending on the nature and scale of the programme, stakeholders might be policy-makers, the programme developers, trainers, teachers, students and school administrative staff. Each of these groups may also be potential audiences for the evaluation report, together with others such as educational researchers, those involved in curriculum development, text-book authors, parents and school governing bodies. It is worth noting that one way of helping to identify the questions of interest to stakeholders and audiences is, where feasible, to interview representatives of each group in order to gather their views on what they see as the issues and priorities.

Boxes 5.7 and 5.8 provide templates for identifying the stakeholders and audiences for an evaluation, and the questions of interest to them. Boxes 5.9 and 5.10 illustrate how the templates might be used to start identifying the questions of interest to stakeholders and audiences for the evaluation of the support programme for underachieving students.

Box 5.7   Template for identifying stakeholders and questions of interest to them

- The key stakeholders in the programme are . . .

For each group of stakeholders in turn:
- Priorities for this group are likely to be . . .
- The questions of most interest to this group are therefore . . .

Box 5.8   Using the template to start identifying stakeholders in the support programme and questions of interest to them

The key stakeholders in the programme are

1   the senior management teams in the schools;
2   the teachers involved in the programme;
3   the students involved in the programme;
4   the parents of the students;
5   the administrative staff involved in the setting up and maintaining of the database.

The senior management team
Priorities for this group are likely to focus on the effects the programme is having on students' performance, and how much time teaching and administrative staff spend running the programme.

The questions of most interest to this group are therefore

- What improvements are seen in students' performance in classwork, tests and examinations?
- How much time do teachers spend with students?
- How much administrative time is spent on the programme by teaching and administrative staff?

The students
Priorities for this group are likely to focus on the perceived usefulness of the 'Progress diary'.

The questions of most interest to this group are therefore

- How much time does it take students to complete the 'Progress diary' and keep it up-to-date?
- How helpful is the 'Progress diary' as a means of recording work and progress?
- How do parents of students respond to the 'Progress diary'?
- What effects does the 'Progress diary' have on how students feel about their work and progress?

Box 5.9 Template for identifying audiences and questions of interest to them

- The key audiences for the evaluation report on the programme are . . .

For each of these audiences in turn:
- Priorities for this group are likely to be . . .
- The questions of most interest to this group are therefore . . .

With any new programme, decisions need to be taken about which aspects will be evaluated and what questions will be asked about each of these aspects. Where a new programme is comparatively small in scale, there will be limits to the number of possibilities for evaluation. However, large-scale, multifaceted innovations, such as those associated with some curriculum development projects, open up a very substantial evaluation agenda. Decisions about which questions to include in an evaluation need to be taken in relation to the resources available in terms of time and money, and to the constraints which may operate relating to deadlines and access to potential data sources.

Deciding on the evaluation questions

All evaluation studies involve asking questions about a new programme and gathering data to inform the answers. Section 2 has described a number of ways in which evaluation questions may be characterized, depending on their nature and focus, and shown that they may be:

- causal – seeking to establish links between cause and effect;
- non-causal – seeking to gather information;
and focus on one or more of

- the goals of the new programme (the intended curriculum)
- what teachers and students are doing in the classroom during the new programme (the implemented curriculum);

Box 5.10   Using the template to start identifying audiences for a report on the support programme and questions of interest to them

The key audiences for the evaluation report on the programme are:

1   the senior management teams in the schools;
2   the teachers involved in the programme;
3   the students involved in the programme;
4   the parents of the students;
5   the administrative staff involved in the setting up and maintaining of the database;
6   the schools' governing bodies;
7   other schools interested in helping underachieving students.

The teachers
Priorities for this group are likely to be the ease with which they can use the programme materials, the time demands associated with the programme, how students respond in the individual monthly reviews, and the perceived or actual benefits in terms of students' responses in class and performance in tests and examinations.

The questions of most interest to this group are therefore:

- What do I think of the programme materials?
- How am I finding the individual monthly reviews?
- What changes have I seen in my students' behaviour in lessons?
- What changes are there in my students' performance in tests and examinations?
- Is what I am doing a good investment of my time?

- the outcomes of the new programme (the achieved curriculum).

An evaluation which emphasizes the summative dimension will be seeking to formulate questions of the causal type and focus on goals and outcomes, whereas an evaluation which emphasizes the formative dimension will be seeking to formulate questions of the non-causal type and explore what is happening during an innovation.

Evaluations typically address between one and five or six main evaluation questions. Arriving at these questions involves the following steps:

- producing a list of all the questions which have been identified through an examination of goals;
- adding to the list all the questions which have emerged through a consideration of the concerns and issues of importance to stakeholders and audiences;
- making a judgement about the relative importance of the questions and eliminating those which are of lower priority in terms of the interests of stakeholders and audiences;
- assessing the practical considerations associated with answering the questions and eliminating those which are impractical;
- grouping the remaining questions under a number of themes to give the main evaluation questions.

In the example evaluation . . .

Questions which form the focus of the evaluation of the support programme for underachieving students are likely to fall into five main areas: effects on students' performance in classwork, tests and examinations; how teachers use the materials provided for the programme; the training and support provided for teachers; the time involved in running and administering the programme; and teachers', students' and parents' views of the programme.

Box 5.11 identifies some possible overall evaluation questions for the example evaluation.

There is a mix of causal questions (1, 2, 3 and 8) and non-causal questions (4, 5, 6 and 7). The causal questions generally focus on the intended and achieved curriculum, whilst the non-causal questions address aspects of the implemented curriculum. The final question (8) concerns all three aspects of the programme.

Box 5.11   Possible evaluation questions in the example evaluation

1   What are the effects of the programme on students' performance in tests and examinations?
2   How effective was the programme for different students?
3   Which aspects of the programme were most effective?
4   What are the experiences of teachers and students participating in the programme?
5   How does what is happening in practice match the goals of the programme?
6   What barriers are being encountered in implementing the programme, and what strategies are being used to overcome these?
7   What are the views of teachers and students on the value of the programme?
8   Which aspects of the programme appear to be most effective in helping those involved meet the goals of the programme and why?

What use will be made of the findings?

The purpose of any evaluation needs to be clear: why is it being undertaken and to what use will the findings be put? As described in Section 1, Cronbach (1963) suggested that evaluation data can be used for one or more of three purposes: making *decisions about course improvements*, making *decisions about individuals* (such as students' needs and staff professional development), and *administrative regulation* (i.e. related to accountability and the effectiveness with which schools and teachers are operating). Within this, a number of the different audiences for an evaluation report could be involved in decisions, including those who have developed the materials being evaluated, those using them, and external agencies such as funders/policy-makers.

In the example evaluation . . .

In the example evaluation of the support programme for underachieving students, the purposes of the evaluation are primarily to do with making decisions about improvements in provision and making decisions about individuals, particularly in relation to students' needs in terms of support with their work, and the training needs for staff. One possible outcome is that the effects of the programme are not judged to justify the time and effort involved, and the programme would be withdrawn. Some elements of administrative regulation are also present, in that the programme is aimed at improving school effectiveness in relation to performance in national tests and examinations.

What types of data will be collected to help answer the evaluation questions?

Evaluation studies normally gather two principal types of data, *quantitative* data and *qualitative* data (see Glossary).

In the example evaluation . . .

A small-scale evaluation study such as in the example of the support programme for underachieving students is likely to gather a range of qualitative data from both staff and students. Additionally, the pooling of results from the four schools involved might permit some limited statistical analysis of test and examination marks.

What techniques will be used to gather the data?

A variety of techniques may be used for gathering evaluation data. These have been described in Section 4.

In the example evaluation . . .

Techniques used to gather data in the example evaluation are likely to include drawing on information in documents and existing databases to collect information on test and examination results, interviews with teachers and students and, possibly, with administrative staff, and questionnaires sent to students and, possibly, their parents. Focus groups could also be considered for gathering data from parents, teachers (both within or across schools) and students.

Who will gather the data?

Evaluations are normally undertaken by members of one – or occasionally more than one – of the following groups:

- external agencies;
- those implementing the programme (teacher-evaluators);
- those involved in developing the programme.

The traditional approach to evaluation, particularly summative evaluation, has been to employ an external evaluator to undertake the work. Teacher involvement has been limited to the contribution of data to the study as a user of the programme materials or as one of the audiences for the evaluation report. However, growth of teacher involvement in local and national curriculum development projects has seen teachers playing an increasingly active role in evaluation, both in evaluating their own and colleagues' work in the classroom and in contributing to decision-making on the curriculum in their departments and schools.

The involvement in evaluation of teacher-evaluators and those developing the programme raises the issue of the objectivity of the data collected. Underpinning this is the concern that both those involved in the development of a programme and those using the programme – particularly those users who have been involved in the decision to adopt it – have a vested interest in gathering evidence to suggest the programme is fulfilling its goals. This is certainly a legitimate concern, but one which can be addressed by appropriate planning. An important element of any research, including evaluation, is bringing critical distance to what is being researched: in the formulation of the questions, in the design of the study, in the ways in which data are gathered, analysed and reported, and in identifying potential limitations and improvements. Part of this critical reflection involves examining the views and assumptions that the researcher brings to the work, and taking steps to minimize any potential bias which might be introduced into the research. Whilst external evaluators are less involved in a programme, it would be wrong to assume that they are objective, neutral observers of events who do not bring the own views and assumptions to an evaluation. However, there is a stronger obligation on teacher-evaluators and evaluators involved in the development of a programme to acknowledge and address issues related to potential bias in their reports.

In the example evaluation . . .

In the case of the example small-scale evaluation of the support programme for underachieving students, the staff most closely involved will almost certainly be hoping to see some improvement in students' achievements arising from the time and effort expended by the schools and staff in developing and implementing the programme. Therefore, a teacher-evaluator would need to acknowledge their own role and interest in the programme. Ideally, the evaluation would involve gathering data from staff who were using the programme, but who had not been involved in the decision to adopt it or in the design of the materials.

What ethical considerations need to be addressed?

The nature of evaluation means that it can be seen as a potentially threatening activity by those being evaluated. It is therefore very important that ethical considerations are addressed when undertaking an evaluation. The guiding principle is that participants should be treated fairly, honestly, and with consideration, respect and appreciation. In practice this means that the following will need to be addressed.

- Access to data sources needs to be negotiated. This may include seeking permission from appropriate authorities (such as headteachers and governing bodies) to undertake the work, agreeing with teachers how data will be collected in classrooms, and asking parents' permission for their children to be involved.
- Everyone participating in the evaluation should do so having given their *informed consent*. This means they should be aware of the nature and purpose of the evaluation and of who will have access to its findings.
- There should be no attempt to deceive participants by withholding information from them, for example, by not declaring fully the aims of the evaluation.
- Permission needs to be obtained before looking at documents, files and other paperwork.
- Permission needs to be obtained from the teachers involved if they are to be observed in their classrooms.
- Permission needs to be obtained from participants for data they have provided to be included in any report.
- The confidentiality of participants should be maintained throughout the evaluation and in the writing of the report. This means making sure that information obtained from one respondent is not passed on to other respondents, and that anonymity is preserved where feasible. (This may not be possible in small-scale case-study evaluations.)
- Accounts and conclusions should be negotiated. Participants should be provided with the opportunity to read and to

comment on the fairness and accuracy of descriptions of their work, such as lesson observations or interview transcripts. Participants should also be provided with the opportunity to comment on a draft of the report before it is finalized.

- The right of the evaluator to report the work should be retained.

One of the most potentially sensitive issues in educational evaluation concerns the final two points in this list. The general principle is that evaluators should provide opportunities for participants to satisfy themselves that the contents of the report are accurate, fair, relevant, and not reported in a way which is potentially embarrassing. If these conditions are met, then the evaluators have the right to report the data in the way they think best. Undertaking an evaluation in a spirit of openness is the most effective way of minimizing problems in reporting.

As ethical considerations are so important in educational evaluation, a number of publications exist which offer advice on appropriate procedures and actions. A useful document to consult is *Ethical Guidelines for Educational Research* (BERA, 1992), produced by the British Educational Research Association (BERA).

In the example evaluation . . .

In the case of the example small-scale evaluation of the support programme for underachieving students, a number of ethical issues are likely to need to be addressed. A teacher-evaluator has the advantages of knowing most of the participants and having ready access to data sources, although appropriate formal permission still needs to be obtained for access to these sources. This will include getting permission from the headteacher and parents, if data are to be gathered from students, as is very likely to be the case. As the study is comparatively small in scale, matters to do with confidentiality will need to be negotiated particularly carefully, as it is unlikely that anonymity can be preserved fully for all participants.

How will the evaluation be reported?

An evaluation plan has to take into account the ways in which the study will be reported. In producing the final report of an evaluation, a number of points need to be considered. These include:

- the extent to which one report is suitable for the needs of all the audiences, or whether different, shorter reports tailored for particular audiences are desirable (and whether there is sufficient time and resources to produce several versions);
- the best ways of structuring the information in the report;
- the need to ensure that any conclusions and recommendations are clearly linked to evidence gathered in the evaluation, and that the status of the evidence is made clear;
- that ethical considerations relating to reporting have been sensitively and appropriately addressed.

In essence, the report has to communicate to others clearly, concisely and comprehensibly what has been learned and how it was learned. The general advice for an evaluation report is that it should be short, avoiding lengthy and detailed descriptions of methodology and large sections of descriptive data. Box 5.12 provides a template.

Most evaluation reports begin with an executive summary, of one or two pages in length, containing the questions addressed, the essential findings, the conclusions and recommendations, together with brief reasons for being able to have confidence in the conclusions and recommendations. An important point to remember about the executive summary is that it may well be the only part of the report certain audiences read, and it should therefore focus on the key aspects of the evaluation.

One problem which often exercises those writing evaluation

Box 5.12   Template for an evaluation report

An evaluation report is likely to contain the following main sections:

- an executive summary;
- background: to include a description of the programme and its goals, and identification of the evaluation questions;
- methodology: the strategies and techniques employed to gather the evaluation data;
- data presentation, analysis and interpretation;
- an appendix or appendices containing all the evaluation instruments.

---

reports, particularly where large quantities of qualitative data are involved, concerns the balance between description, analysis and interpretation. The advice offered by Patton (2002) is helpful:

> Sufficient description and quotation should be provided to allow the reader to enter into the situation and thoughts of the people represented in the report . . . The purpose of analysis is to organize description so that it is manageable. Description is balanced by analysis and leads to inter-pretation. An interesting and reasonable report provides sufficient description to allow the reader to understand the basis for an interpretation and sufficient interpretation to allow the reader to appreciate the description.
>
> (2002, 503–4)

Useful features to include in an evaluation report which will help readers relate to the material include quotations, vignettes (short descriptions of typical instances) and examples of good practice.

Summary

This section has drawn on the ideas in previous sections and applied them to the design of a hypothetical evaluation. It has shown that planning an effective evaluation involves consideration of the following areas:

- the form of the evaluation (the summative and/or formative dimensions);
- practical issues (such as the time and money available);
- the questions to be addressed in the evaluation;
- the purpose of the evaluation;
- the types of data to be collected;
- the techniques used to collect the data;
- who will collect the data;
- ethical considerations;
- the way in which the evaluation will be reported.

6

Evaluation in Practice: Some Examples of Studies

This section looks at three examples of evaluation, drawing on the questions in Box 5.1 as a framework for describing and discussing the studies. The intention is that these examples will provide illustrations of the planning process, and those interested in the findings should consult the evaluation reports themselves.

Example 1: A new science course for non-science specialists

What was being evaluated?

This example draws on material in the report, 'Breaking the mould: teaching science for public understanding' (Osborne *et al.*, 2002). The programme being evaluated was a new science course, 'Science for public understanding', developed for use with 16–18 year-olds in the UK. These students are in the post-compulsory and pre-university phase of education. The course is optional, and leads to an external qualification at Advanced Supplementary (AS) level.

What form did the evaluation take?

The evaluation took the form of a survey of teachers and students using the programme (in 55 schools), and case studies of practice in nine of the schools. The study was designed around the framework of Robitaille *et al.* (see Section 2) which seeks to explore links between the intended, implemented and achieved curriculum.

What questions did the evaluation address?

The evaluation set out to look at the intended curriculum, the implemented curriculum and the attained curriculum. Specifically, the questions addressed were:

- How have the teachers implemented this new science course and what difficulties have they encountered?
- How have the students responded to this new science curriculum and what have they learned?

What use was made of the findings?

The intention of the evaluation was to provide a set of recommendations, based on an evaluation of the strengths and weaknesses of the course. These recommendations served two purposes: to improve the existing course, and to advise those developing other courses of a similar nature on appropriate actions and strategies.

What types of data were collected to help answer the evaluation questions?

The evaluation gathered a mix of quantitative and qualitative data, with the majority being of the latter type.

What techniques were used to gather the data?

Data were gathered using the following techniques:

- a questionnaire which surveyed teachers in all 55 schools using the course, seeking basic data such as teachers' ages, backgrounds, reasons for choosing the course and opinions of it. This questionnaire was used to identify the sample of schools used for the case study visits;

- a questionnaire which surveyed all teachers in all 55 schools using the course, seeking more detailed information about teaching strategies and other aspects of the course such as marketing and decisions on uptake;
- semi-structured interviews with 20 teachers to explore aspects including their views about the strengths and weaknesses of the course, difficulties encountered when teaching it, managerial issues, their views on the value of the course, and their perceived professional development needs;
- observation of 27 lessons taught by 10 teachers to capture the range of contexts in which the course was being taught, and the practice of a range of teachers;
- a questionnaire used with a sample of students (around 30% of the 800 taking the course) to explore their reason for taking the course, their expectations of the course, their views on the style of teaching, and their likes and dislikes;
- semi-structured interviews with 20 students to find out how the course had informed and developed their interest in science, what effect it had on their understanding of the major ideas about science covered in the course, and why they had chosen the course;
- an analysis of a random sample (10%) of students' examination scripts to look at how they had answered questions.

Who gathered the data?

Data were gathered by external evaluators.

How was the evaluation reported?

The evaluation was reported in a 92-page document (Osborne *et al.*, 2002), which began with a summary of the study, its main conclusions and principal recommendations before reporting the detail of the work. Information about the research methods and instruments was provided in appendices.

Commentary

This example provides a good illustration of a multi-method approach to evaluation. The evaluators are explicit in their reports about the need for such an approach in the case of this evaluation:

> The questions posed by this study required data which were a mix of factual answers ... [and] deeper insights and explanations. ... The research therefore required a mix of quantitative survey methodologies ... and qualitative interviews and case studies ...
>
> (2002, 82)

The evaluation contained both formative and summative dimensions, in that its purpose was to inform future developments in the course and reach judgements about its effects. In order to do this, a range of strategies and techniques was employed to gather the data. The structure of the report is such that the key aspects of the evaluation are easy to identify and assimilate.

Example 2: A programme aimed at accelerating cognitive development

What was being evaluated?

This example looks at the evaluation of a programme which has received considerable attention in the last decade, the Cognitive Acceleration through Science Education (CASE) project (Adey and Shayer, 1994; Shayer, 1999; Adey, 2000).

What form did the evaluation take?

This evaluation is particularly interesting as it is one of a comparatively limited number of studies which employs a controlled experiment in the evaluation design. The experiment began with nine schools and 24 classes, randomly allocated as twelve control and twelve experimental groups, and with each school containing at least one control and experimental group. These groups were matched as closely as possible in terms of students' ability. In the experimental classes, the teachers used 30 lessons aimed at developing thinking skills in students aged 11 and 12 over a period of two years. In some cases, a teacher was overseeing both experimental and control groups. In total, there were 190 students in the experimental groups and 208 in the control groups.

What questions did the evaluation address?

The evaluation set out to answer the question: what are the effects on lower secondary level students' performance in tests of cognitive ability when they experience a programme aimed at accelerating cognitive ability?

What use was made of the findings?

The intention of the evaluation was to gather data on the effects of the CASE materials with a view to making them more widely available should they prove to raise levels of attainment.

What types of data were collected to help answer the evaluation questions?

The main emphasis of the evaluation was on gathering quantitative data.

What techniques were used to gather the data?

The principal data gathered came from information on students' levels of performance in the following:

- the Piagetian Reasoning Tasks, a test of levels of cognitive development, used at three points in the two-year period;

- a standard science achievement test, used at three points in the two-year period;
- school examination results;
- public examination results at 16+ (General Certificate of Secondary Education, GCSE), three or four years after experiencing the programme.

Who gathered the data?

The majority of the data was gathered by those who developed the materials.

How was the evaluation reported?

The evaluation has been very widely reported in a number of articles in both academic and practitioner journals, and as chapters in books (including Adey and Shayer, 1994; Shayer, 1999; Adey, 2000).

Commentary

This evaluation illustrates some of the challenges associated with using experimental approaches in educational evaluation. The researchers worked very hard to get as close as possible to a true experimental design, but had to operate within the constraints of the classes into which students had already been grouped by their schools. One reason for the CASE work receiving so much attention was the superior performance in examinations at 16+ of students in the experimental groups in science, mathematics and English. It also appears to be the case that one strength of the work lies in its 'hard' numerical data, which has proved very persuasive to other teachers and resulted in their schools adopting the materials. However, it has also resulted in other researchers questioning the validity of the claims made for the materials, and those developing the CASE materials have had to engage in vigorous defence of their position. It seems that even when (or, perhaps, particularly when) experiments appear to offer concrete evidence of 'what works', their findings are open to debate.

Example 3: A thinking skills programme for primary-school students

What was being evaluated?

The programme being evaluated was a thinking skills programme developed by a teacher-researcher for use with primary-age students (Chang and Kyriacou, 1996).

What form did the evaluation take?

The evaluation took the form of a case study of practice in the researcher's school. Aspects of experimental design (a quasi-experiment) were introduced into the study, in that a comparison was made between the group experiencing the programme and another group.

What questions did the evaluation address?

The evaluation set out to answer the question: what are the effects of using materials aimed at developing thinking skills in primary-age children on their critical thinking abilities and attainment in lessons?

What use was made of the findings?

The intention of the evaluation was to decide whether to implement the programme throughout the school.

What types of data were collected to help answer the evaluation questions?

The evaluation gathered a mix of quantitative and qualitative data.

What techniques were used to gather the data?

Data were gathered through observation and interviews with students. The former data were collected by another teacher, who observed the lessons and was also interviewed to gather information about views on what had been observed. Other sources of data were provided by video-recording the lessons, and the researcher kept field notes throughout the teaching of the programme. Additionally, a test of critical thinking abilities was given to the experimental group and to a control group, before and after the programme was taught.

Who gathered the data?

Data were gathered by the teacher who designed and taught the programme and by an additional teacher who assisted in the gathering of observation data.

How was the evaluation reported?

The evaluation was reported in a journal paper (Chang and Kyriacou, 1996).

Commentary

This evaluation illustrates a common multi-method format in a small-scale study undertaken by a teacher-researcher, i.e. a case study where several sources of data are gathered for the purposes of triangulation. In this case, it was also possible to use a quasi-experimental design to add strength to any claims being made about the effects of the programme.

Summary

This section has presented three examples of evaluation studies:

- a multi-method evaluation, with both formative and summative dimensions, of a medium-to-large-scale innovation;

- an evaluation which is largely summative in approach and linked to an experimental design drawing on a large sample;
- a multi-method evaluation of a small-scale innovation, undertaken by a teacher-researcher.

These examples have illustrated the very different ways in which principles may be put into practice when undertaking educational evaluation.

Glossary

Where an item is highlighted in **bold**, it has an individual entry in the glossary.

Action research

Action research is a **research strategy** which has become increasingly popular with small-scale research in educational settings, because it is about finding practical solutions to practical problems. A central feature of action research is that the researcher is involved in the research process. Much **practitioner research** therefore takes the form of action research. A typical action research study has three main stages: identifying a problem, identifying and implementing a course of action, and evaluating the success of the action. Action research is often described as a cyclical process, as evaluation may well lead to further action.

Case study

Case studies as a **research strategy** have become very widely used in social research, and are highly popular in **small-scale research** undertaken by practitioner-researchers. They focus on one aspect of a particular situation and use a range of research techniques to explore the situation in depth, with a view to identifying the various processes at work within it. A criticism of case studies concerns the extent to which their findings can be generalized – features which exert a strong influence in one context may not be present in another. However, case studies are normally judged by their **relatability**, rather than their **generalizability** – a good case study will be reported in such a way that the members of a similar group will be able to identify with the problems and issues being reported, and to draw on these in order to see ways of solving similar problems in their own situation.

Data audit trail

A data audit trail is a concise summary of each step taken in collecting and analysing data. It allows someone reading a report of the work to see exactly what data were collected and the steps taken in the analysis.

Design experiment

Design experiments draw on the evaluation approaches used in technology and engineering, which aim to explore how a product, developed to solve a particular problem, performs in selected situations. In educational contexts, the 'product' being tested could be a new programme. A design experiment evaluates the effects of the programme in a limited number of settings.

Document study

This **research technique** involves a detailed study of documents relevant to a study. Such documents might take a number of forms, including test results and existing databases of information, policy statements and accounts of innovations.

Empirical research

Empirical research involves data collection through direct interaction with the data sources via **questionnaires**, **interviews** and **observation**.

Ethnography

Ethnography is a **research strategy** which has its origins in the work of anthropologists studying aspects of a particular group in depth. It involves the researcher becoming a member of the group being studied in order to share their experiences and try to understand why members of the group act in particular ways. As with case studies, there are problems with the reliability of ethnographic studies. Whilst there are some examples of researchers joining staff in a school, the nature of much educational research, with its focus on pupils, makes ethnographic research difficult in educational contexts!

Experiment
Experiments are used as a **research strategy** in order to test out theories or discover new relationships. The key feature of experiments is that they involve identifying and isolating individual aspects of a situation (variables), making changes, and observing the effects in detail. Experiments are normally associated with summative evaluations and the gathering of quantitative data. Experiments are designed to test a hypothesis. They involve setting up an experimental group, who will experience some form of 'treatment' (such as a new programme), and a control group, who will not. The idea is that if the two groups are well-matched, then any differences in the outcomes observed can be attributed with confidence to the 'treatment' that the experimental group experienced.

There are two common experimental designs: (i) the *true experimental design* (or **randomized controlled trial, RCT**) which has matched control and experimental groups, where equivalence has been achieved allocating members randomly to either group; (ii) the *quasi-experimental design* which has non-equivalent control groups but which is as similar as possible in key characteristics. Evaluations may also make use of *pre-experimental design* which involves assessing or testing a group on a particular measure (the pre-test), introducing a new programme, and then reassessing the group using the same measure (the post-test). However, the lack of control of variables means that any effects are open to question.

Two factors have made experiments comparatively rare in educational contexts. First, controlling variables often presents problems in educational settings. Second, conducting experiments in educational settings raises ethical issues. Changes to curriculum provision are made in the hope that they will lead to improvements, and experiments therefore involve depriving one group of something which it is hoped will be beneficial, although this outcome is by no means certain and cannot be judged in advance.

Focus group

Focus groups are a comparatively new **research technique** in education. They are used to gather views and opinions by giving participants a topic or a series of questions to discuss. The researcher's main role in the discussion is simply to listen. One reason for the increasing popularity of focus groups is that, like **interviews**, they can be used to explore topics in depth but, unlike interviews, they can gather a relatively large amount of data in a short time.

Formative evaluation

Formative evaluation (sometimes called process evaluation) is carried out during an innovation in order to inform the development process whilst changes can still be made.

Generalizability

Generalizability refers to the extent to which the findings in one situation can be applied to others.

Interviews

Interviews are a very popular **research technique** as they enable research questions to be explored in depth by going beyond factual matters to seek views and explanations. They are often used in conjunction with **questionnaires**, either to identify aspects to be explored in a questionnaire, or to probe the responses given in questionnaires in more depth.

Large-scale study

The term large-scale study tends to be associated with projects with a number of researchers, external funding, and which involve the collection of data from a large number of people in a range of locations.

Observation

Observation is used as a **research technique** when data on actual practices are required. Like **questionnaires**, observation generates factual information rather than explanations.

Practitioner research

A practitioner researcher – a teacher in educational contexts – is simultaneously working in a particular field and researching an aspect of practice.

Qualitative data

Qualitative data are non-numeric in nature, making use of words in the form of descriptions. Such data are normally gathered through **interviews**, **focus groups** or **observation**.

Quantitative data

Quantitative data make use of numbers, which can be analysed by statistical techniques if drawn from a wide sample. Such techniques allow researchers to establish the extent to which their findings are statistically significant, i.e. not down to mere chance. Quantitative data are normally gathered by **questionnaires** and from test results or existing databases.

Questionnaire

Questionnaires are a very popular **research technique** as they provide a cost-effective means of gathering a wide range of fairly straightforward, factual information. They are usually better at answering questions about 'what' and 'how', rather than 'why'.

Randomized Controlled Trial (RCT)

Randomized Controlled Trials are experiments which test alternative courses of action, such as different teaching approaches. Sometimes the trial involves testing an intervention against what would have happened had it not been used, and sometimes different interventions are compared. A key aspect of an RCT is that, although members are allocated randomly to groups (see **sample**), the groups being compared are as similar in composition as possible.

Relatabilty
Relatability is a term often used in connection with case studies, where generalizability is an issue. Rather than make more general claims for the findings, a researcher provides sufficient detail for readers to judge how far the outcomes might apply to their own situation.

Reliability
Data are said to be reliable if repeating the technique gives the same result again. Undertaking trials of research instruments is an important step in ensuring reliability. (See also **validity**.)

Research strategy
There are four (occasionally five) strategies used in educational research: **action research**, **case study**, **ethnography** (although this can present problems – see entry for ethnography), **experiment** and **survey**.

Research techniques
Five techniques for gathering data are common in educational research: **document study**, **interviews** (with **focus groups** as a variation), **observation** and **questionnaires**.

Sample
In educational research it is often not possible to collect data from all the participants. In this case, a sample has to be identified. Two common types of sample are the random sample and the stratified (quota) sample. A *random sample* is drawn in such a way that every member of the whole population (which may be pupils in a class or school) has an equal chance of being selected

– for example by drawing names from a hat. A *stratified* or *quota sample* is one which matches certain features of the population. For example, the sample might need to reflect the proportion of males/females or the number of urban/suburban/rural schools in the population as a whole. Subjects are therefore first grouped, and then chosen randomly from each group.

Small-scale study
A small-scale study is likely to be one undertaken by a single researcher, and involve collecting from a limited number of sources, such as a teacher collecting data in their own school as part of a higher degree research study.

Summative evaluation
Summative evaluation (sometimes called outcome or impact evaluation) is carried out at the end of an innovation to assess its impact by comparing aims with outcomes.

Survey
The survey is a **research technique** which aims to collect data from a representative sample group with a view to presenting the findings as being applicable to a much larger group. Surveys tend to be associated with **large-scale studies** and make use of **questionnaires**, often to gather **quantitative data**. The major advantage of surveys lies in the breadth and inclusive nature of the data collected. They are less good at yielding explanations for events. Surveys are often employed when one aim of the research is to be able to make comparisons between different groups.

Triangulation
In the strictest sense of its meaning, triangulation involves gathering data from three sources, and often using more than one method, to strengthen claims resulting from a study. In practice, the term tends to indicate that more than one source has been used to provide the data.

Trustworthiness
Trustworthiness is a term often used in qualitative research as an alternative to **reliability** and **validity**. Data are described as trustworthy if they are seen as credible by those reading reports of the work.

Validity
Data are said to be valid if they measure what they claim to be measuring. (See also **reliability**.)

Variables
A variable is a characteristic which varies from one situation to another. Some variables are quantitative (i.e. numerical), such as age or test scores, whereas others may be qualitative (i.e. non-numerical), such as gender. An experiment involves making a change in one variable – the independent variable – and monitoring the effects of that change on another variable – the dependent variable. For example, groups of pupils might be taught in either single-sex or mixed-sex groupings (the independent variable), and the effects on pupil performance in tests monitored.

Appendix:
Selected further reading on research methods and data analysis

In addition to the books in the Continuum Research Methods Series, the following books provide good introductions to educational research:

Bell, J. (1999) *Doing Your Research Project: A Guide for First-time Researchers in Education and Social Science. 3rd edn.* Buckingham: Open University Press.

Blaxter, L., Hughes, C. and Tight, M. (1996) *How to Research.* Buckingham: Open University Press.

Cohen, L., Manion, L. and Morrison, K. (2000) *Research Methods in Education. 5th edn.* London: Routledge.

Denscombe, M. (1998) *The Good Research Guide.* Buckingham: Open University Press.

Drever, E. (1995) *Using Semi-structured Interviews in Small-scale Research: A Teacher's Guide.* Edinburgh: The Scottish Council for Research in Education.

Hopkins, D. (1989) *Evaluation for School Development.* Buckingham: Open University Press.

Hopkins, D. (2002) *A Teacher's Guide to Classroom Research. 3rd edn.* Buckingham: Open University Press.

Munn, P. and Drever, E. (1995) *Using Questionnaires in Small-scale Research: A Teachers' Guide. 2nd edn.* Edinburgh: The Scottish Council for Research in Education.

Simpson, M. and Tuson, J. (1995) *Using Observations in Small-scale Research.* Edinburgh: Scottish Council for Research in Education.

Wellington, J. (2000) *Educational Research: Contemporary Issues and Practical Approaches.* London: Continuum.

Bibliography

Adey, P. (2000) Science teaching and the development of intelligence. In M. Monk and J. Osborne (eds) *Good Practice in Science Teaching: What Research Has to Say*. Buckingham: Open University Press.

Adey, P. and Shayer, M. (1994) *Really Raising Standards: Cognitive Intervention and Academic Achievement*. London: Routledge.

Atkinson, P. and Delamont, S. (1993) Bread and dreams or bread and circuses? A critique of 'case study' research in education. In M. Hammersley (ed.) *Controversies in Classroom Research. 2nd Edition*. Buckingham: Open University Press.

Bassey, M. (1981) Pedagogic research: On the relative merits of search for generalization and study of single events. *Oxford Review of Education*, 7 (1), 73–94.

Bloom, B. (1970) Towards a theory of testing which included measurement – evaluation – testing. In M. Wittrock and D. Wiley (eds) *The Evaluation of Instruction: Issues and Problems*. New York: Holt, Rinehart and Winston.

Boruch, R. (1997) *Randomized Experimentation for Planning and Evaluation: A Practical Guide*. London: Sage Publications.

British Educational Research Association [BERA] (1992) *Ethical Guidelines for Educational Research*. Edinburgh: British Educational Research Association.

Brown, A. (1992) Design experiments: Theoretical and methodological challenges in creating complex interventions in classroom settings. *The Journal of the Learning Sciences*, 2 (2), 141–78.

Chang, L. W. and Kyriacou, K. (1996) Teaching thinking skills to primary school pupils in Taiwan. *Education Section Review*, 20 (1), 28–30.

Collins, A. (1993) Towards a design science of education. In

E. Scanlon and T. O'Shea (eds) *New Directions in Educational Technology*. New York: Springer Verlag.

Cronbach, L. (1963) Course improvement through evaluation. *Teachers College Record*, 64, 672–83. Reprinted in M. Golby, J. Greenwald and R. West (eds) (1975) *Curriculum Design*. London: Croom Helm.

Cronbach, L., Ambron, S., Dornbusch, S., Hess, R., Hornik, R, Phillips, D., Walter, D. and Weiner, S. (1980) *Toward Reform of Program Evaluation*. San Francisco: Jossey Bass.

Davies, H., Nutley, S. and Tilley, N. (2000) Debates on the role of experimentation. In H. Davies, S. Nutley and P. Smith (eds) *What Works?: Evidence-based Policy and Practice in the Public Services*. Bristol: Policy Press.

Delamont, S. (1978) Sociology in the classroom. In L. Barton and R. Meighan (eds) *Sociological Interpretations of Schools and Classrooms*. Driffield: Nafferton Books.

Department for Education and Employment/Welsh Office [DfEE/WO] (1989) *Science in the National Curriculum*. London: HMSO.

EPPI-Centre (2002) *Core Keywording Strategy*. London: Social Science Research Unit, Institute of Education, University of London.

Fitz-Gibbon, C. (2000) Education: realising the potential. In H. Davies, S. Nutley and P. Smith (eds) *What Works? Evidence-based Policy and Practice in Public Services*. Bristol: Policy Press.

Fitz-Gibbon, C. and Morris, L. (1987) *How to Design a Programme Evaluation*. London: Sage Publications.

Fullan, M. (1982) *The Meaning of Educational Change*. Toronto: OISE Press.

Fullan, M. (1983) Evaluating program implementation. *Curriculum Inquiry*, 13, 214–27.

Fullan, M. (2001) *The New Meaning of Educational Change. 3rd edition*. London: Cassell.

Hall, G., Wallace, R. and Dossett, W. (1973) *A Developmental Conceptualization of the Adoption Process within Educational Institutions*. Austin, Texas: Research and Development Center for Teacher Education, The University of Texas at Austin. The questionnaire is available for purchase from: South West Educational Development Laboratory [SEDL] (2002) *The Stages of Concern Questionnaire*. *www.sedl.org/pubs/catalog/items/cbam*

Hamilton, D. (1976) *Curriculum Evaluation*. London: Open Books.

Hargreaves, D. (1996) Teaching as a research-based profession:

Possibilities and prospects. *Teacher Training Agency Annual Lecture.* London: The Teacher Training Agency (TTA).

Harland, J. and Kinder, K. (1997) Teachers' continuing professional development: Framing a model of outcomes. *British Journal of In-service Education,* 23 (1), 71–84.

Hillage, L., Pearson, R., Anderson, A. and Tamkin, P. (1998) *Excellence in Research on Schools.* Brighton: Institute for Employment Studies.

Hopkins, D. (1989) *Evaluation for School Development.* Milton Keynes: Open University Press.

Hord, S. (1987) *Evaluating Educational Innovation.* London: Croom Helm.

Jenkins, D. (1976) *Open University Course E203, Curriculum Design and Development. Unit 19: Curriculum Evaluation.* Milton Keynes: The Open University.

Joyce, B. and Showers, B. (1980) Improving in-service training: The messages of research. *Educational Leadership,* 37, 379–85.

Joyce, B. and Showers, B. (1995) *Student Achievement through Staff Development.* White Plains, New York: Longman.

Kerr, J. (1968) *Changing the Curriculum.* London: University of London Press.

Kinder, K. and Harland, J. (1991) *The Impact of INSET: The Case of Primary Science.* Slough: National Foundation for Educational Research [NFER].

Kinder, K., Harland, J. and Wootten, M. (1991) *The Impact of School Focused INSET on Classroom Practice.* Slough: National Foundation for Educational Research [NFER].

Lawton, D. (1980) *The Politics of the School Curriculum.* London: Routledge and Kegan Paul.

Lawton, D. (1983) *Curriculum Studies and Educational Planning.* London: Hodder and Stoughton.

Lincoln, Y. and Guba, E. (1985) *Naturalistic Inquiry.* London: Sage Publications.

MacDonald, B. (1976) Evaluation and the control of education. In D. Tawney (ed.) *Curriculum Evaluation Today: Trends and Implications.* London: MacMillan.

Miles, M. and Huberman, M. (1994) *Qualitative Data Analysis: An Expanded Sourcebook. 2nd edn.* London: Sage.

Millar, R. (2002) Evaluation science curriculum innovation: issues and perspectives. Paper presented at the York-IPN International Symposium, 9–11 May 2002, University of York.

Nevo, D. (1986) Conceptualisation of educational evaluation. In E. House (ed.) *New Directions in Educational Evaluation*. London: The Falmer Press.

Norris, N. (1990) *Understanding Educational Evaluation*. London: Kegan Page.

Oakley, A. (2000) *Experiments in Knowing*. Cambridge: Polity Press.

Osborne, J., Duschl, R. and Fairbrother, R. (2002) *Breaking the Mould: Teaching Science for Public Understanding*. London: The Nuffield Foundation.

Parlett, M. and Hamilton, D. (1972) Evaluation as illumination: A new approach to the study of innovative programmes. *Occasional Paper No. 9*, Edinburgh: Centre for Research in the Educational Sciences, University of Edinburgh. Reprinted (1976) in D. Tawney (ed.) *Curriculum Evaluation Today: Trends and Implications*. London: Macmillan.

Patton, M. (2002) *Qualitative Research and Evaluation Methods. 3rd edn*. Thousand Oaks, California: Sage.

Robitaille, D., McKnight, C., Schmidt, W., Britton, E., Raizen, S and Nicol, C. (1993) Curriculum frameworks for mathematics and science. *TIMSS Monograph, No. 1*. Vancouver: Pacific Educational Press.

Scriven, M. (1973) Goal-free evaluation. In E. House (ed.) *School Evaluation: The Politics and Process*. Berkeley, California: McCutchan Publishing Corporation.

Scriven, M. (1967) The methodology of evaluation. In R. Stake (ed.) *Perspectives of Curriculum Evaluation*. American Educational Research Association. Chicago: Rand McNally.

Shavelson, R. and Towne, L. (eds) (2001) *Scientific Inquiry in Education*. Washington, DC: National Academy Press.

Shayer, M. (1999) Cognitive acceleration through science education II: Its effects and scope. *International Journal of Science Education*, 21 (8), 883–902.

Smith, M. and Glass, G. (1987) *Research and Evaluation in Education and the Social Sciences*. Englewood Cliffs, New Jersey: Prentice Hall.

Stake, R. (1967) The countenance of educational evaluation. *Teachers College Record*, 68, 523–40.

Stake, R. (1986) Evaluating educational programmes. In D. Hopkins (ed.) *Inservice Training and Educational Development*. London: Croom Helm.

Stenhouse, L. (1975) *An Introduction to Curriculum Research and Development*. Oxford: Heinemann Educational Books.

Tooley, J. and Darbey, D. (1998) *Educational Research: A Critique. A Survey of Published Educational Research*. London: Office for Standards in Education (Ofsted).

Torgerson, C. and Torgerson, D. (2001) The need for randomized controlled trials in educational research. *British Journal of Educational Studies*, 49 (3), 316–28.

Tyler, R. (1949) *Basic Principles of Curriculum and Instruction*. Chicago: University of Chicago Press.

Index